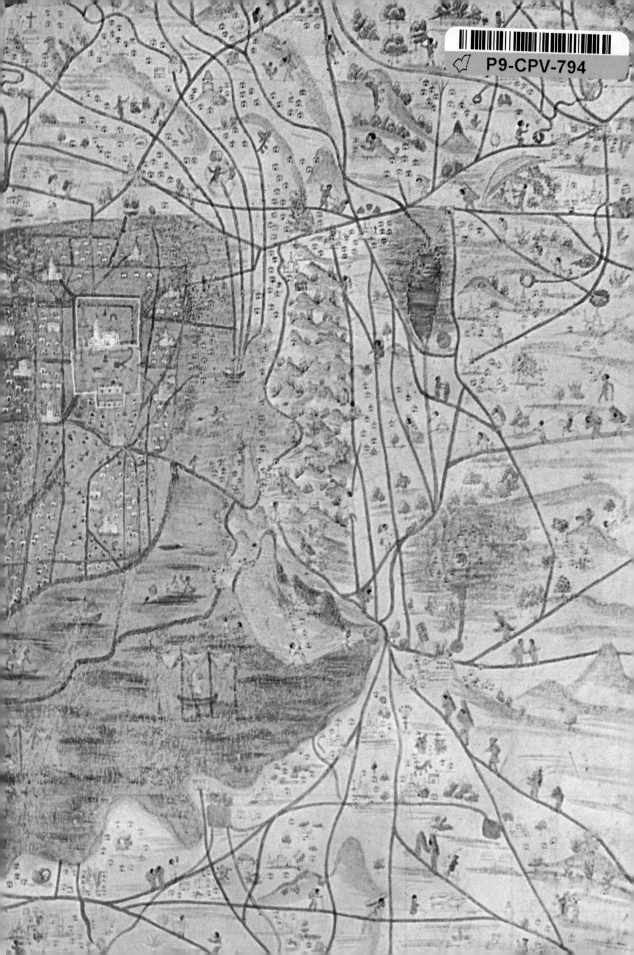

There are a number of HORIZON CARAVEL BOOKS published each year. Titles now available are:

CONSTANTINOPLE, CITY ON THE GOLDEN HORN
LORENZO DE' MEDICI AND THE RENAISSANCE
MASTER BUILDERS OF THE MIDDLE AGES
PIZARRO AND THE CONQUEST OF PERU
FERDINAND AND ISABELLA
CHARLEMAGNE
CHARLES DARWIN AND THE ORIGIN OF SPECIES
RUSSIA IN REVOLUTION
DESERT WAR IN NORTH AFRICA
THE BATTLE OF WATERLOO
THE HOLY LAND IN THE TIME OF JESUS
THE SPANISH ARMADA
BUILDING THE SUEZ CANAL
MOUNTAIN CONQUEST
PHARAOHS OF EGYPT
LEONARDO DA VINCI
THE FRENCH REVOLUTION
CORTES AND THE AZTEC CONQUEST
CAESAR
THE UNIVERSE OF GALILEO AND NEWTON
THE VIKINGS
MARCO POLO'S ADVENTURES IN CHINA
SHAKESPEARE'S ENGLAND
CAPTAIN COOK AND THE SOUTH PACIFIC
THE SEARCH FOR EARLY MAN
JOAN OF ARC
EXPLORATION OF AFRICA
NELSON AND THE AGE OF FIGHTING SAIL
ALEXANDER THE GREAT
RUSSIA UNDER THE CZARS
HEROES OF POLAR EXPLORATION
KNIGHTS OF THE CRUSADES

American Heritage also publishes AMERICAN HERITAGE JUNIOR LIBRARY books, a similar series on American history. Titles now available are:

THE BATTLE OF THE BULGE
THE BATTLE OF YORKTOWN
THE HISTORY OF THE ATOMIC BOMB
TO THE PACIFIC WITH LEWIS AND CLARK
THEODORE ROOSEVELT, THE STRENUOUS LIFE
GEORGE WASHINGTON AND THE MAKING OF A NATION
CAPTAINS OF INDUSTRY
CARRIER WAR IN THE PACIFIC
JAMESTOWN: FIRST ENGLISH COLONY
AMERICANS IN SPACE
ABRAHAM LINCOLN IN PEACE AND WAR
AIR WAR AGAINST HITLER'S GERMANY
IRONCLADS OF THE CIVIL WAR
THE ERIE CANAL
THE MANY WORLDS OF BENJAMIN FRANKLIN
COMMODORE PERRY IN JAPAN
THE BATTLE OF GETTYSBURG
ANDREW JACKSON, SOLDIER AND STATESMAN
ADVENTURES IN THE WILDERNESS
LEXINGTON, CONCORD AND BUNKER HILL
CLIPPER SHIPS AND CAPTAINS
D-DAY, THE INVASION OF EUROPE
WESTWARD ON THE OREGON TRAIL
THE FRENCH AND INDIAN WARS
GREAT DAYS OF THE CIRCUS
STEAMBOATS ON THE MISSISSIPPI
COWBOYS AND CATTLE COUNTRY
TEXAS AND THE WAR WITH MEXICO
THE PILGRIMS AND PLYMOUTH COLONY
THE CALIFORNIA GOLD RUSH
PIRATES OF THE SPANISH MAIN
TRAPPERS AND MOUNTAIN MEN
MEN OF SCIENCE AND INVENTION
NAVAL BATTLES AND HEROES
THOMAS JEFFERSON AND HIS WORLD
DISCOVERERS OF THE NEW WORLD
RAILROADS IN THE DAYS OF STEAM
INDIANS OF THE PLAINS
THE STORY OF YANKEE WHALING

A HORIZON CARAVEL BOOK

CORTES

AND THE AZTEC CONQUEST

By the Editors of
HORIZON MAGAZINE

Author
IRWIN R. BLACKER

Consultant
GORDON EKHOLM

Curator of Mexican Archaeology, American Museum of Natural History

ILLUSTRATED WITH MANY PAINTINGS, DRAWINGS,
AND ARTIFACTS OF THE PERIOD

Published by American Heritage Publishing Co., Inc.
Book Trade and Institutional Distribution by
Harper & Row

FOURTH PRINTING

Library of Congress Catalogue Card Number: 65–11533
© 1965 by American Heritage Publishing Co., Inc., 551 Fifth Avenue, New York 17,
New York. All rights reserved under Berne and Pan-American Copyright Conventions.
Trademark CARAVEL registered United States Patent Office

FOREWORD

To the gold-hungry Spaniards Hernando Cortes was a brash upstart who had gone off to invade Mexico without sufficient authority. To the devout Aztecs he was a long-absent god who had returned to Mexico City to fulfill a legendary promise.

In three years (1519–1522) this bold and fortunate conquistador, leading a few hundred Spanish soldiers, overcame a centuries-old empire that could put tens of thousands of warriors into the field. Even after his godlike reputation had been shattered, and his horses and cannon were no longer regarded as supernatural, his ruthless daring took him on to victory. Yet in the end his prize was not the gold that he had sought, but the destruction of an entire civilization.

The story of Cortes thus involves not only the confrontation of two colorful cultures (with a representative of Europe's grandest monarch meeting the mighty Montezuma) but also the violent death of a great empire. Only recently has the work of archaeologists and scholars in Mexico been combined with traditional Spanish and Indian sources to give a detailed picture of those blood-thirsty native conquerors who, in turn, were conquered by Cortes. Bolstering the factual record are the Aztecs' own illustrated histories (left) and dramatic Spanish paintings that were made in later decades to memorialize the triumphs of the conquistadors.

Against this composite background of art, science, and scholarship, the heroic figure of Hernando Cortes stands forth with ever greater clarity. It was he who arrogantly battered open the doors of the New World, the model for a new generation of conquistadors who would begin the exploration of this continent with careless courage.

THE EDITORS

Montezuma sent artists to record Cortes' arrival in Mexico. This copy of one such drawing shows the Spaniard with cross, banner, and sword. Beneath him and the envoy greeting him are glyphs—the Aztecs' symbolic writing.

7

At right is the coat of arms given Cortes by his king; on the shield Mexico is shown as a towered city.

COVER: *Before the rise of the Aztecs or the coming of Cortes, an Indian artist painted this blazing sun with demons surrounding it.*

TITLE PAGE: *The Aztec god Tez-catlipoca could see everything on earth in the mirror on his right foot.*

FRONT ENDSHEET: *A native artist drew this view of Mexico City, with Aztecs engaged in hunting and fishing, soon after the 1520 conquest.*

BACK ENDSHEET: *Two centuries later, a Spanish artist made this anachronistic picture of the Aztec capital, including cows and ships.*

CONTENTS

GOLD IN THE WEST

On February 8, 1517, one hundred and ten Spanish adventurers in three ships put to sea from a small port on the north coast of Cuba. A breeze rose from the east, and their pilot—Antonio Alaminos, who had sailed with Columbus—pointed the prows toward the setting sun. Although the adventurers had heard that land lay to the west, none of them knew the winds in the area, the currents, or the depth of the water, but they sailed on until suddenly they were caught up in a raging storm. For two days and two nights huge waves battered the three ships. Then the skies cleared, and they continued westward.

Twenty-one days after they left Cuba, they sighted a

An Indian spy posted in a tree observes the approach of a Spanish ship to the Mexican coast in 1518. This event was recorded by the contemporary Spanish historian Diego Durán, whose book was illustrated with many simple, vivid drawings.

Treasure was what the Spanish invaders of the New World sought. To their surprise, when they found gold, it was in the form of such intricately wrought native objects as these. The large piece (about 2½ inches long) is a gold pendant designed to resemble a rattlesnake's tail; the smaller pieces are a bell and an eagle head, also of gold.

headland in the distance (Cape Catoche in modern-day Mexico), and on a rise beyond the coast, they could make out a great city. In two unrewarding decades of colonizing the New World and searching for the fabled riches of the Indies, no Spaniard had ever seen a larger or more promising objective.

The two smaller vessels moved boldly toward the shore and were met by ten Indian canoes. In one of the canoes was a native chieftain, a cacique, who beckoned the Spaniards to come ashore. Led by their captain, Francisco de Córdoba, twenty-five men formed ranks on the beach and prepared to march inland. They had proceeded only a short distance toward the city when they were suddenly ambushed by Indians hidden in the brush. The first volley of Indian arrows wounded fifteen Spaniards, and then the two forces closed with each other. The Spanish soldiers, with their heavy plate armor and steel swords, grappled with the natives, who wore only heavy cotton padding and wielded lances.

The unequal battle was over almost as quickly as it started. The Indians fled the field, leaving fifteen of their dead behind. Córdoba and his men moved forward eagerly; from where they stood they could see a small open square and three houses built of masonry. As evidence of an advanced native culture, these intriguing buildings—the first masonry structures found in the New World—excited the Spaniards to hope that they were on the threshold of even greater treasures.

With combined curiosity and cupidity, Córdoba and his companions entered the houses. Here they found pottery idols, some with the faces of demons, some with the faces of women. They also found a wooden chest with tiny gold and copper ornaments. Convinced even by this small find that they had made an important discovery, they returned to their ships and continued exploring along the coast toward the setting sun.

What they had unknowingly discovered was the Maya civilization of the peninsula of Yucatán. By accident, Córdoba and his men had stumbled upon a people who have been called the Greeks of the Western Hemisphere.

Before the birth of Christ, the Maya civilization was taking form in what is now Guatemala, in highland and lowland regions to the south and west of the Yucatán city that Córdoba had sighted. According to the vague historical picture that archaeological research is now slowly providing, Maya civilization reached the culmination of

TEXT CONTINUED ON PAGE 17

Diego Velásquez sailed to the New World with Columbus in 1493 and soon became governor of Cuba as well as the most ambitious promoter of gold-hunting expeditions in the Caribbean. One of the three expeditions he sent out from Cuba in the early 1500's is pictured at left—perhaps that of Francisco de Córdoba. All the expeditions met with bloody resistance from the Indians, whose bows and clubs were no match for Spanish steel and gunpowder (below).

PALACES OF THE MAYA

By a strange accident of history, the gold-hungry Spaniards happened to strike the New World in one of its richest cultural sites. The Yucatán peninsula and the mainland areas behind it (in present-day Mexico, Guatemala, and Honduras) made up the homeland of the ancient Maya—whose magnificent civilization flourished for six centuries before A.D. 1000. Throughout this vast, lush area are the ruined pyramids and palaces of a vanished culture; the Spaniards discovered some of these monuments, others have been found more recently. Maya society was based on a religion of many gods, some fierce and insatiable, and was ruled by priests and nobles. But why the lofty temples of the Maya were often deliberately destroyed and

why their great religious centers were abandoned are questions that may never be answered. Copán, where the massive, snaggle-toothed stone head at right was recently discovered among over-growing trees, was one of the Maya centers that was abandoned after the "classic period" (A.D. 300–900). Perhaps the most rewarding Maya site for modern tourists is Chichén Itzá in Yucatan (below). Like Copán, it was apparently abandoned but then re-occupied and overrun by a breed of bloodthirsty invaders from central Mexico. Encouraged by a glimpse of the heights reached by this Indian culture, the Spanish explorers hoped to find an even mightier civilization that had not yet declined, where a river of gold still flowed into the city.

NORMAN CARVER

16

The ships of Cortes and other early Spanish conquerors (conquistadors) were generally three-masted carracks like the large vessel in the 1540 woodcut at right. Only later were the slender galleons developed which carried gold swiftly from New Spain ("Neufue Espaigne" on the 1555 map at left) to the Spanish court. The peninsula of Yucatán is at left of center on the map and is labeled "Lucatan."

TEXT CONTINUED FROM PAGE 12

its development in the six centuries between A.D. 300 and 900 and then began to decline. At their height the Maya were in many ways the most civilized people in the Americas. They had a calendar more precise than any known in Europe until more than a half century after Córdoba's voyage. The massive stone and concrete buildings they constructed for their numerous ceremonial centers displayed an impressive architectural skill. They engineered aqueducts and roads that still exist, and there is also archaeological evidence that the Maya succeeded in building stone bridges, reservoirs, and elaborate underground passages.

The Maya were extraordinary artists in stone and wood sculpture and in painting. They were the only people in the New World to have an effective system of writing, a by-product of their consuming interest in mathematics and astronomy—sciences in which they excelled. They were also among the few people anywhere in the world at that time whose food supply was so abundant that they had an opportunity to develop their civilization more fully.

Late in their history, around the beginning of the eleventh century, the Maya lost much of the vigor and discipline that had regulated their former growth, and Yucatán was occupied by dissident and warring groups. It was one of these remaining tribes that Córdoba and his men had discovered on that fateful day in 1517.

After their first conflict with the Maya Indians, Córdoba's force sailed down the west coast of Yucatán for fifteen days until they saw another large town near a great bay. Here they dropped anchor and went ashore to fill

17

Ponce de León discovered Florida in 1513, but he did not attempt to conquer it until 1521—then he was fatally wounded by an Indian's poisoned arrow. In the eighteenth-century view of that incident above, the Spaniards are shown in three ranks, loading and firing musket-like weapons called harquebuses.

their water casks. They were again attacked by the Maya, and this encounter proved to be even bloodier. The surrounded Spaniards received no quarter; from the beginning the battle went against Córdoba. And then more Maya warriors joined the conflict, violently swinging their flint-edged wooden swords. As the battle raged, Córdoba was wounded ten times. Soon, fifty of the Spaniards were dead, and those who still lived were wounded and weary. With their last efforts the adventurers broke out of the circle of natives, and fighting shoulder to shoulder, they struggled back toward the beach, where their boats were waiting. The natives continued to press them, and as Córdoba and his men reached the water, arrows showered over them. The Indians waded into the surf after them even as the smallest of the ships drew in close to shore and the Spaniards clambered aboard. At last the sails were raised, and the ships put to sea.

Afterward, Córdoba and his companions realized that the battle, for all of its fury, had lasted but an hour. Slowly the adventurers looked about and counted their dead— they had lost no more than fifty men. But in the next few days they cast five additional companions, dead from wounds and thirst, into the sea. The natives called the place where they fought Champotón, but the pilots marked it on their charts as the Coast of the Disastrous Battle.

The men dressed their wounds and cursed the pilot

18

Alaminos because once more he had taken them to a well populated and stoutly defended part of the peninsula of Yucatán. And because there were no longer enough able seamen remaining to handle the ships, they brought the vessels together off the coast, stripped the smallest, and burned its hull. Then they divided the ablebodied sailors into two crews for the remaining ships and went in search of fresh water. After a few days they paused at one salty creek, but finding nothing to drink, they sailed on. Rather than return to Cuba by the route they had come, Alaminos suggested they sail northward and home by way of Florida, where he knew they could find fresh water.

Along the Florida coast they stopped for water, and as they were returning to their ships they were attacked a third time. Fighting furiously, Córdoba's men drove back the Indians who had swarmed down upon them. This time they left twenty dead Indians on the shore or in the water. However, four Spaniards were wounded, and Alaminos himself was badly injured. Unable any longer to fight new battles, the adventurers turned their two ships homeward.

At last they reached the coast of Cuba. It had been a rugged expedition, during which many good men had lost their lives. Francisco de Córdoba and three more soldiers eventually died from their wounds. But despite their losses, the small band had discovered something they thought was important—rich lands to the westward, lands that no white man had ever before explored.

The fame of the skillfully designed gold ornaments that Córdoba's expedition found and brought to Cuba soon spread throughout the islands and eventually reached Spain. Writing half a century later, Bernal Díaz del Castillo, who had sailed with Córdoba, stated, "It was said that better lands had never been discovered in the world."

As soon as he heard the report of the expedition, Governor Diego Velásquez of Cuba, an old soldier who had first come to the New World with Columbus, prepared to send a second and stronger fleet to explore Yucatán. He bought two additional ships with his own money, rehired Alaminos as a pilot, and selected his captains. Two of those he chose—Pedro de Alvarado and Francisco de Montejo—were to play important roles in the years that followed. To these he added Alonzo de Avila and his own cousin, twenty-eight-year-old Juan de Grijalva, who was appointed captain general. As soon as the story about the riches to be won in the newly discovered lands was heard,

Chronicler of Córdoba's expedition was Bernal Díaz del Castillo (above), who later marched to the interior of Mexico with Cortes. In a page from Díaz's manuscript (at top) he describes how the ships set out from Cuba for Yucatán in 1517.

volunteers rushed to join the new expedition. In a short time, 240 soldiers and settlers had signed on.

After attending a mass said in their honor, they sailed for Yucatán early in April, 1518. Eighteen days later they paused at a small island called Cozumel and then pushed on. By May 3 they were again in the neighborhood of Champotón, where Córdoba's expedition had been so badly mauled.

As the fleet neared land, the Spaniards could see rows of Maya warriors lining the shore, ready for battle. Grijalva and his men put on their armor; then they lowered their landing boats and prepared to meet the Indians. This time the Spaniards carried falconets—small but powerful cannon that could easily be hauled over the beaches. As the boats crossed the surf, the Indians bombarded the Spaniards with arrows, wounding half of them. But Grijalva and his men did not hesitate. They rowed into shore, grounded their boats, and opened fire. This second battle at Champotón was almost as bloody as the first. Seven of the invaders were killed on the beach, and Juan de Grijalva was wounded three times. But the Maya could not hold their ground, and they fled into the nearby swamps.

BOTH: N.Y. PUBLIC LIBRARY, RARE BOOK DIVISION

Falconets were light cannon about four feet long designed for shipboard use. When an expedition such as Grijalva's disembarked, the falconets were hauled overland on runners or wheels. In the sixteenth-century drawing at left, soldiers with harquebuses have just fired, covering the falconets, which have been loaded and are now ready to discharge. In the print at right, a portrait of Grijalva is set into a scene of his encounter with the Indians at the second battle of Champotón; the other scene is an Indian festival in front of a temple.

The Spaniards stopped only to tend their wounded and bury their dead before marching into Champotón. There they stayed for three days before putting to sea once more. They coasted along the Yucatán peninsula during the day but had to anchor by night for fear of the shoals and the reefs. Finally, they came to a broad-mouthed river that they named after their captain general. From the decks of their ships they could see Maya forces numbering into the thousands collecting on the shore. Undaunted, Grijalva had his fleet draw closer, and the Indians came out in fifty war canoes to meet them.

Grijalva tried to parley with the Maya through an interpreter. For a moment all was tense. Then the spokesman for the Indians said that his people knew about the first battle at Champotón, and if the strangers intended to fight, the Indians had twenty-four thousand soldiers ready to war with them. Grijalva explained that all he wanted was to trade, and he displayed the glass beads he had brought. The Indians agreed to tell their chiefs what the strangers wanted and to return as soon as possible with the answer.

The chiefs agreed to Grijalva's proposal, and the next

Grijalva pelea con los Indios

In this romantic lithograph, Governor Velásquez is urging Cortes to sail forth and conquer Mexico. Bernal Díaz implies that Cortes was selected to head the expedition because he could be trusted not to reveal Velásquez's plan to loot the mainland rather than colonize it.

day he and his soldiers met with the Maya traders, who brought food and jewels that they wanted to exchange for the Spanish trinkets. There was only a small amount of gold, and when the strangers asked for more the Indians pointed toward the sunset and exclaimed, "*Mejico, Mejico.*" The Spaniards had no way of knowing what *Mejico* meant, but they were satisfied that there was more gold in that direction.

When the trading was done, Grijalva put to sea. Sailing along the coast, the Spaniards were startled to find a large number of Indians waving white banners and signaling for them to come ashore. What Grijalva did not know was that word of their arrival on the coast had been sent inland by messenger and that the local ruler had given orders for his subjects to trade with the strangers. Accepting the invitation, Grijalva went ashore, and for six days he traded cheap beads to the Maya for sixteen thousand dollars worth of gold and jewels—the largest single collection of treasure yet acquired in the New World.

Grijalva also took possession of the land in the name of Spain. Satisfied that there was no more to be gained, the fleet sailed on, pausing once at a small island on which the explorers saw from their ships a number of masonry buildings and a temple. They went ashore and entered the temple where they found the bodies of five Indians whose chests had been ripped open and whose thighs and arms had been cut off in sacrifice to the native idols upon the altars. The walls were covered with blood. This place the Spaniards called the Island of Sacrifices.

Grijalva sent Captain Alvarado back to Cuba with the fastest ship and all of the treasure they had gathered. With the rest of the small fleet, he planned to continue his explorations. However, the weather soon turned against him, and the ships began to leak. Finally, he abandoned the effort and turned homeward.

Governor Velásquez took one look at the treasure that Alvarado spread before him and immediately began to prepare another expedition without waiting for the return of Grijalva. His motives for this swift action may have been personal; the governor yielded to no man in the Caribbean in his desire for wealth. But he also had official reasons: for the first time it looked as if the Spanish investment in the New World might show that vast profit that Columbus, the Great Admiral, had promised.

In the twenty-five years following the discovery of the Indies, Spain poured money into expeditions that probed the coasts of both North and South America. But there had been little success. Numerous fleets put out each year without finding anything of value. Yet despite all the failures, despite all the ships that returned empty or foundered in storms, more and more Spaniards shipped westward in their small, square-rigged caravels. The voyage was difficult; the men slept under the open sky, when the weather was clear, or below in the rat-infested, leaky holds when there were storms. The food was usually cold, and after a few weeks it crawled with worms, and the water turned green. But still the men came to the New World looking for lands to conquer. They yearned to become conquistadors—conquerers—but so far they had found no lands worthy of conquest.

Cuba became their base. Some of the men, disappointed in their search, turned to farming. Others remained in the small villages while they waited for their opportunity. The voyages of Córdoba and Grijalva appeared to point a way, and they were eager to take it.

From these adventurers, Governor Velásquez had no trouble recruiting men for his third expedition. This one was to become the most important ever to set foot upon the mainland and one in which two great civilizations were to be locked in mortal conflict—a conflict that would end with the destruction of an empire. To command this expedition, Velásquez selected a young planter who would in time become his enemy. His name was Hernando Cortes.

The Spanish court painter Alonso Sánchez Coello painted this portrait of Cortes to show how the young Spaniard looked at the time of his departure for the New World.

MAXIMILIANVS I IMP.
ARCHIDVX AVSTRIÆ.
DVX BVRGVNDIÆ.

PHILIPPVS HISP. REX. I.
ARCHIDVX AVSTRIÆ.

MARIA DVCISSA
BVRGVNDIÆ MAX: VXC

FERDINANDVS I IMP.
ARCHIDVX AVSTRIÆ.

CAROLVS V. IMP.
ARCHIDVX AVSTRIÆ.

LVDOVICVS REX
HVNG. MAS.

24

II

THE GOVERNOR'S CHOICE

There were many men who wanted to command the third expedition, which was to be larger, and more important, than its predecessors. The four ships of Grijalva were careened and readied for the return to Yucatán, and Velásquez arranged for six more to join the fleet. Some men held that Grijalva should be given the new command, but it went instead to Hernando Cortes, the *alcalde*, or mayor, of the small plantation town of San Juan de Baracoa. Cortes had served under Governor Velásquez in the expedition that had subjugated Cuba in 1511. And during the subsequent years he had lived off the income of a plantation that had been placed in his custody by Velásquez.

Born the son of a poor country gentleman at Medellín, Spain, in 1485, the youthful Cortes had been educated for two years at the University of Salamanca. However, his temperament was such that he returned home restless, without a vocation, and ready for adventure. For a time he considered going to Italy as a soldier, but in 1504 he sailed for the New World.

Popular and influential in the Cuban colony, Cortes was eager to lead the expedition. Whether he was appointed because of political influence or because Velásquez respected him, the expedition soon became the personal project of Cortes. Once he was in command, no one ever successfully challenged his authority.

Cortes immediately began to scour the island for arms, gunpowder, armor, crossbows, and any other munitions he could assemble. What money he could borrow on his plantation and his future he poured into equipping the expedition. It seemed clear to him that any and all debts would be paid

Charles, the young boy with the jutting jaw at the bottom of the painting opposite, became Holy Roman Emperor in 1519 because of his father's family, the Hapsburgs; but he inherited Spain and the New World through his mother's parents, Ferdinand and Isabella—shown above receiving Columbus.

off by the wealth that he could pick up on the mainland.

Velásquez nervously watched more than 350 soldiers gather at Santiago de Cuba that winter. And as he listened to his jealous relatives whispering in his ear about the growing power of Cortes, he had second thoughts about his choice of a leader. When Cortes was finally warned that Velásquez was thinking of removing him from command, he resolved to outmaneuver the hesitant governor. Immediately, he ordered all of his officers, sailors, and soldiers aboard their ships. Then, before Velásquez could stammer out a new order, Cortes strode into his office, bade him goodbye, and sailed off to the Cuban port of Trinidad, where he hoped he would be beyond the governor's reach.

At Trinidad, Cortes continued his recruiting, adding to his company the five Alvarado brothers as well as Cristóbal de Olid and the young Gonzalo de Sandoval, who in time was to become a great warrior and Cortes' most intimate friend. Pedro de Alvarado, Olid, and Sandoval eventually became the senior captains under Cortes, whose title of captain general gave him sufficient power to muster men and materials without further authority. In Trinidad, Cortes was also able to purchase one more ship for his fleet, bringing the total to eleven.

While Cortes waited for weapons and armor to be forged and arrows to be made, Velásquez sent a messenger to the mayor of Trinidad with orders to relieve Cortes of his command—under no circumstances was the mayor to allow the fleet to sail. However, Cortes had quickly won the loyalty of most of his men, even though some were relatives and friends of Velásquez's. Also, there were too few soldiers in Trinidad to stop the headstrong captain general. Though the mayor was a close relative of Velásquez's, he timidly ignored the orders of his superior.

Cortes completed his recruiting in Trinidad and sailed for old Havana in southern Cuba, where he made his final preparations and gathered what horses he could. Because they were expensive and in short supply, Cortes was only able to purchase sixteen mounts, but these horses were so important to the expedition that fifty years later Bernal Díaz del Castillo, the chronicler who sailed with both Córdoba and Cortes, could recall each animal, its personality, its color, and its owner.

Meanwhile, Velásquez was growing increasingly concerned about his inability to control Cortes, and he rushed messengers to old Havana with orders for his lieutenant there to seize Cortes and return him to Santiago de Cuba.

This Spanish gunner fires a crude harquebus by setting off the powder in the touch hole with a smoldering slow match. The match was held in an S-shaped pivot on the side of the gun, beside the barrel.

Spanish infantry consisted mostly of gunners, seen above with matches in their left hands. While they went through the slow process of reloading, they were guarded by armored halberdiers (top row, center).

Again the captain general learned of the plan, and again resolved to ignore the orders. Instead of obeying the governor, Cortes sent him a flattering letter with the news that the fleet would sail the next day.

On February 10, 1519, the adventurers climbed aboard their ships and sailed for the small island of Cozumel off the coast of Yucátan. Cortes made one stop along the way at Cape San Antonio. There he ordered a muster so he could learn how many men he actually had, what condition they were in, and what they could do. When all were counted, he discovered he had 508 fighting men as well as 100 shipmasters, pilots, and sailors. There were sixteen horses, although not all of them were suited for use in battle. Thirty-two men were armed with crossbows, and thirteen others had firearms called harquebuses. In addition to several brass guns, there were four falconets.

His muster completed, Cortes continued on to Cozumel. When he arrived on the island, he began to search for an interpreter. The few native prisoners his men could take there repeated over and over one word—*Castilian.*

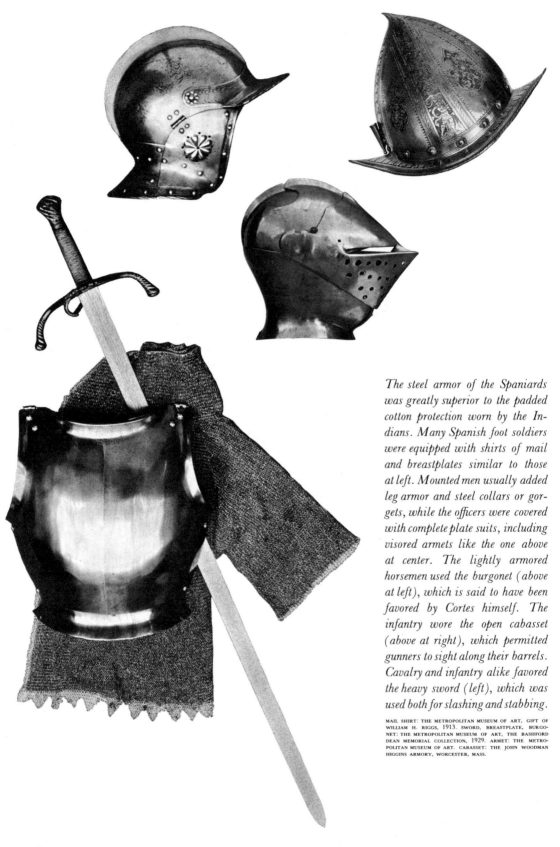

The steel armor of the Spaniards was greatly superior to the padded cotton protection worn by the Indians. Many Spanish foot soldiers were equipped with shirts of mail and breastplates similar to those at left. Mounted men usually added leg armor and steel collars or gorgets, while the officers were covered with complete plate suits, including visored armets like the one above at center. The lightly armored horsemen used the burgonet (above at left), which is said to have been favored by Cortes himself. The infantry wore the open cabasset (above at right), which permitted gunners to sight along their barrels. Cavalry and infantry alike favored the heavy sword (left), which was used both for slashing and stabbing.

MAIL SHIRT: THE METROPOLITAN MUSEUM OF ART, GIFT OF WILLIAM H. RIGGS, 1913. SWORD, BREASTPLATE, BURGONET: THE METROPOLITAN MUSEUM OF ART, THE BASHFORD DEAN MEMORIAL COLLECTION, 1929. ARMET: THE METROPOLITAN MUSEUM OF ART. CABASSET: THE JOHN WOODMAN HIGGINS ARMORY, WORCESTER, MASS.

Since this was a name the Spaniards used to refer to themselves, Cortes concluded that the natives could only have learned it from a Spaniard. To find him, Cortes sent his small boats to the mainland with written messages to be left with the natives, who were to take them to any European castaway on the shores of Yucatán. Within two weeks Cortes' messages produced Jerónimo de Aguilar, who had been shipwrecked on the coast eight years before. Gratefully, he came across to Cozumel and joined Cortes.

At last Cortes was ready for his landing upon the mainland. On March 4, 1519, the fleet left Cozumel. The weather was good on the first day, and the high-pooped ships scudded along before the wind. But at nightfall a vicious headwind scattered the vessels and threatened to drive them back onto Cuba's dark shore. Fortunately the fierce winds blew themselves out that very night, and the expedition was able to sail westward once more. Finally, on March 12, the fleet dropped anchor at the entrance of the Grijalva River. The larger vessels remained offshore while the smaller ones landed the soldiers at the Cape of Palms, several miles from the town of Tabasco. As Cortes and his men beached their small boats they could see that the river and its banks were swarming with Indians, a number of whom the Spaniards rounded up and questioned. Thus they learned the reason for the natives' great numbers and apparent hostility: the people of Tabasco had been accused of cowardice by their neighbors for having traded with Grijalva on his visit the preceding year; now they were prepared to regain their honor. Where Grijalva had found friends and trade, Cortes faced a battle.

Sending Aguilar forward to explain that he came in peace, Cortes offered to trade with the Tabascans and even tried to buy their friendship. However, the natives warned Aguilar that if the Spaniards advanced beyond the palm trees along the shore, they would attack.

The next day Cortes prepared to occupy the town of Tabasco. He approached it from the river with his small boats and sent a column overland through a narrow pass to enclose the Indians between his two forces. He was not anxious for a fight, and through a messenger he tried one last time to allay the fears of the natives. When this failed, the battle began.

The Tabascans and their allies attacked before the Spaniards could beach their boats, and Cortes had to fight his way ashore through the mud. At length the conquistadors reached the town, where they fought their way from

bloody street to bloody street as the natives refused to abandon their homes. Then the overland column reached the outskirts of Tabasco, and the two Spanish forces were united. Though encircled, the Tabascans refused to yield, and Cortes had to fight for every foot of ground he captured. Finally he gained a large courtyard with three buildings that housed idols. The natives had gathered their valuables there, and when they saw the Spaniards enter the buildings, they gave up the struggle and fled.

Immediately after the natives had retreated, Cortes hacked three slashes into the trunk of a large tree growing in the courtyard and took possession of the land in the name of King Charles I of Spain. He declared that he was prepared to defend this claim against any objections with the sword he held in his own hand. When no one attempted to challenge his dramatic proclamation, he sheathed his sword.

After the ceremony he counted his wounded and found that fourteen were injured. Cortes did what he could to help them and then appointed sentries to watch for any further attack. That night the Spaniards slept in the courtyard with their weapons at their sides. They realized that their control of Tabasco had brought them only a momentary respite.

For the next several days Cortes' captains scouted the countryside, trying without success to establish peaceful contact with the Indians. Then one day a Spanish column was ambushed. During the skirmish, three Indian prisoners were taken, and from them Cortes learned that all of the natives in the nearby area were gathering for a full-scale attack against them. Frustrated and angry at his inability to bring about a peace parley, he decided to face the Indians. On March 25, thirteen days after reaching Tabasco, Cortes fought his second pitched battle.

He called for a two-pronged attack. Leading the cavalry, Cortes moved through the forest in an effort to surprise the enemy while his men formed ranks on an open plain near the town of Cintla. As soon as his soldiers arrived there, a mass of Indians swarmed over the small Spanish force. In the first assault, a fierce barrage of arrows, darts, and stones wounded seventy of the Spaniards. The Spanish

Cortes' objectives were gold, royal recognition, and the advancement of Christianity. The 1530 painting opposite portrays him with a coat of arms granted by the king; above, Spaniards raise a cross in the New World.

guns roared back, and hundreds of Indians fell. Then the two forces closed. The conquistadors hacked away at the Indians with their steel weapons, slowly pushing them back. But the natives were so numerous that their heavy losses seemed to have no effect upon them.

The Spaniards were beginning to tire, and they were impatient for the arrival of Cortes and the cavalry to relieve them. Finally, after an hour of fighting, the horsemen

appeared, attacking the Indians from the rear. The impression created by horses and riders, a sight the Indians had never before seen, and the speed with which the cavalry drove through the enemy lines, broke the attack. The Tabascans panicked and fled. Eight hundred Indians were left dead on the battlefield, while Cortes had lost only two men.

In this battle the basic military pattern of the conquest

This scene from Durán's history of the conquest illustrates an incident that took place on Good Friday, 1519. Cortes (encamped on the coast) is told by Doña Marina, the native princess who became his translator, what has been said by the Indian ambassador at far right.

The twentieth-century artist Diego Rivera painted many scenes of the Spanish conquest. A part of his frieze decorating Cortes' former palace in Cuernavaca, Mexico, is at left: Doña Marina points to gifts that Montezuma's emissaries have brought to Cortes in place of an invitation to the capital.

was established. On one side was a small force of Spaniards; on the other, an overwhelming number of natives. The Spaniards generally wore steel armor, fought with steel swords and with guns and cannons, and they were supported by cavalry. The Indians fought bare-chested, or protected by padded jackets, and carried wicker shields; and they shot stone-tipped arrows or swung wooden swords edged with obsidian.

On the day following the battle, Cortes was visited by a delegation of minor Tabascan chiefs. They were well dressed and they carried fish, birds, and fruit as gifts. First they asked permission to bury their dead, and then they agreed to give Cortes whatever he demanded. He accepted their homage, and the following day the people of Tabasco and the neighboring towns returned with more gifts—golden ornaments, dogs, and ducks.

The Indians also brought with them a number of women slaves whom they gave to Cortes and his officers as presents. One of these slaves was to be more valuable to Cortes than any of the gold. The Spaniards named her Doña Marina. She was a young, highly intelligent princess who had been sold into slavery by her parents. She spoke both the Maya language of the coastal Indians and the Nahuatl language, which was spoken by many peoples of the interior, and she possessed a great facility for all language. Soon Doña Marina became Cortes' chief interpreter.

34

After five days, during which the Spaniards rested and made their first notable attempt to win the Indians to Christianity—they raised a great cross for the Indians to contemplate—Cortes and his men once more boarded their ships and set out to find a rich city along the coast. The wind was fair, and the small fleet hugged the shore, sailing past the Alvarado and the Banderas rivers, where Grijalva had traded beads for gold, past the Island of Sacrifices, where Grijalva's men had seen the bloody altars, and finally anchored off the island of San Juan de Ulúa, in the harbor of present-day Veracruz, on Holy Thursday, 1519. (See map on page 116.)

On Good Friday, Cortes and his expedition disembarked, built a small camp, and made contact with the local Indians, members of a powerful nation called the Aztecs. The next day the Spaniards were visited by an emissary of the Aztecs' great leader, Emperor Montezuma II, whose empire included most of the people in the country called Mexico. Gifts were exchanged, and Cortes fired off his cannons and performed cavalry maneuvers to impress his guests. Later Cortes suggested that he would like to meet with the emperor, and the emissary agreed to carry to Montezuma the message of Cortes and the respects of the Spanish king. During the week that the Spaniards awaited the return of the ambassadors, Cortes sent his ships farther northward along the coast to locate a safe

TEXT CONTINUED ON PAGE 38

Each gift of valuables the Spaniards received from the coastal Indians persuaded the conquistadors that greater riches awaited in the interior. Below, a native delegation gives Cortes a bead necklace.

35

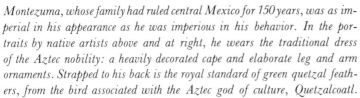

Montezuma, whose family had ruled central Mexico for 150 years, was as imperial in his appearance as he was imperious in his behavior. In the portraits by native artists above and at right, he wears the traditional dress of the Aztec nobility: a heavily decorated cape and elaborate leg and arm ornaments. Strapped to his back is the royal standard of green quetzal feathers, from the bird associated with the Aztec god of culture, Quetzalcoatl.

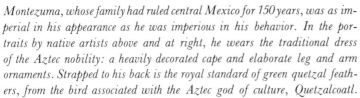

Lienzo de Tlaxcalla, CHAVERO, 1892

Xaltelolco.

Cortes realized that the best way to pry open Montezuma's empire was to seek allies for Spain among the Indian tribes loosely bound to the Aztec federation. In the Spanish painting at right Cortes cements an alliance with a Cempoalan chief by accepting food from his hands. In Tlaxcala, an Indian city-state whose friendship Cortes could not win without many parleys (left) and battles, he was finally able to make a firm alliance against Montezuma.

TEXT CONTINUED FROM PAGE 35

harbor and a place where a fortified town could be built.

Finally, Montezuma's ambassadors returned and politely informed Cortes that under no circumstances could the emperor grant him an audience. They did not go on to explain Montezuma's reason, which was that he feared the rivalry of this strange new visitor from beyond the sea. To soften the refusal, the ambassadors presented the Spanish leader with gifts of gold and some precious stones. The sight of these convinced Cortes and his fellow conquistadors that if they were to take over the riches of the New World, they should first meet with the Aztec ruler. However, Cortes did not have the authority from his own king to treat with royalty, to march in conquest, or even to settle on the mainland. What power he held had been given him by Velásquez, and that was merely to explore, trade, and return.

After a series of secret meetings with his most trusted officers, Cortes set out to improve his political position and remove himself from the authority of Velásquez. He knew enough about Spanish governmental intrigue to see that no independent move would succeed. All power was granted by the king of Spain, and no one could change that fact. It was the king who had appointed Velásquez, and Velásquez who in turn had appointed Cortes.

In the small Spanish camp on the coast, the story soon

Framed by an arching rainbow in this crude drawing of Villa Rica de Vera Cruz are three consecutive events. In the background an Indian sights the Spanish ships; at left sailors unload arms, animals, and supplies; at right Doña Marina questions a native as a clerk takes down the information. An important fourth event is not shown—the deliberate scuttling of Cortes' ships.

passed from soldier to soldier that somehow Velásquez had betrayed them all. Indignantly the soldiers muttered that they did not even have the power to make their own decisions. Soon some of these men asked Cortes to take command of a new settlement and form a new colonial administration that would be loyal to the Crown but free of Velásquez. For a time, Cortes feigned loyalty to the governor who had appointed him and to the instructions he had been given. He pretended to need a great deal of persuasion before he finally allowed himself to be selected

both chief justice of the new colony and captain general —with a fifth share of all gold discovered after the "royal fifth" had been put aside. The agreement was formally set down by the expedition's notary, and Cortes no longer felt that he was obligated in any way to Velásquez.

The political maneuvering done, Cortes and his men set out to build a base of operations on the coast. They found a suitable site for their first permanent community in a vicinity where the natives were relatively friendly. With great care they laid out a town that they called Villa Rica de Vera Cruz—Rich Town of the True Cross—so named because the land was rich and because they had landed on the Holy Friday of the Cross. A pillory was placed in the plaza and a gallows was erected on the edge of town. Then Cortes named a town council and other officials. Everything was done as legally as possible because what they were doing in Mexico would have to be approved by the king in Spain.

However, each step that Cortes and his friends took infuriated the relatives and friends of Velásquez who were part of the expedition. These men were more eager than ever to return to Cuba and re-establish themselves with the governor, whose power was recognized by the king. They did not want to dally in Mexico under the command of a man whom they considered a rebel against established authority. As a consequence, Cortes could wait no longer; he was forced to take immediate action or lose everything he had gained so far. First, and most important, he had to establish contact with Spain, for the final decision about who was to be in command of the Spanish forces on the mainland could be made nowhere but at the court of King Charles.

Gathering up all the gold and the other colorful presents which had been given him by the various chiefs and by the ambassadors of Montezuma, Cortes implored his followers to give up their shares for the time being and use this treasure to impress the king. When he had finally persuaded them, he outfitted the largest ship in his fleet, loaded the treasure aboard, and provisioned the vessel for the voyage to Spain. For this delicate task he assigned fifteen sailors and two men whom he greatly trusted— Alonzo Hernandez Puertocarrero and Francisco de Montejo—as representatives to inform the king what had already been accomplished and how bright the prospects were for the future.

Once his emissaries had sailed, Cortes began to pre-

When the conquistadors built their base at Villa Rica de Vera Cruz, their plan and designs were Spanish, though the craftsmanship was Indian. Here Cempoalan natives help construct the first Spanish buildings in the New World from heavy timbers and yellow clay.

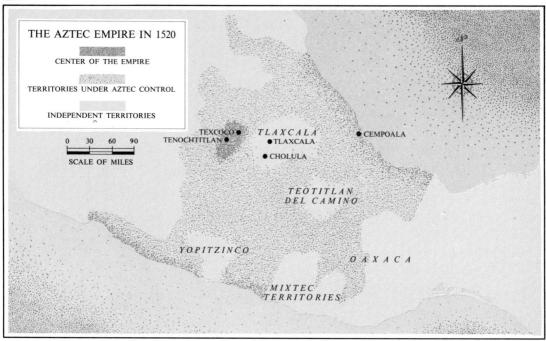

THE AZTEC EMPIRE IN 1520

CENTER OF THE EMPIRE

TERRITORIES UNDER AZTEC CONTROL

INDEPENDENT TERRITORIES

0   30   60   90

SCALE OF MILES

TEXCOCO
TENOCHTITLAN   TLAXCALA   CEMPOALA
•TLAXCALA
•CHOLULA

TEOTITLAN
DEL CAMINO

YOPITZINCO   OAXACA

MIXTEC
TERRITORIES

The Aztec empire consisted of two parts: at the heart, around the vast lakes that existed in the Valley of Mexico in the 1500's, were the city-states ruled directly by Montezuma; beyond these lay the territories of subjugated tribes from whom the Aztecs took as tribute precious metals and slaves.

pare for the march to the city called *Mejico*, or Mexico, the capital about which he had been hearing rumors since his landing. (For pronunciation of Mexican names see Index.)

In the midst of these preparations, several of the followers of Velásquez were making plans to flee the mainland and sail for Cuba. One of their number betrayed his companions to Cortes, who arrested the lot. Two of the conspirators were sentenced to death, a third was to have his feet cut off, and the others were to receive two hundred lashes each. Although the records do not tell whether these harsh sentences were carried out, it is doubtful that Cortes would have been inclined to be merciful, for his chief weapon was the disciplined loyalty of his men.

Cortes had every reason to fear that there would be further dissension from those who still favored Velásquez. Also, there were cowards and sluggards who wanted simply to return home to their Cuban farms or were afraid to risk the long march inland to find the Emperor Montezuma. There was only one way Cortes could prevent their flight; he stripped his fleet of the iron, sails, cord, and equipment and scuttled the ships. He left none of the Spaniards a choice: they would have to remain under his command in Mexico. Those who were too old or ill would remain at Villa Rica de Vera Cruz while the others marched inland.

Before Cortes left the coast for his great overland adventure, he concluded an alliance with the chief of Cempoala and the rulers of other neighboring towns so that the Spanish defenders of Villa Rica de Vera Cruz would have assistance in case of an attack from Cuba.

When all this was done, there seemed to be nothing to keep Cortes from his meeting with Montezuma. In mid-August, 1519, with the help of several hundred Indians, the Spanish column of probably no more than 350 men marched westward from Cempoala. They kept a close formation, sending on before the main body only the scouts and a few foot soldiers. Ahead, somewhere beyond the mountains, lay the capital city of Mexico. And there they would find Montezuma, the emperor who held sway over this vast land.

However, the journey was to take longer than Cortes and those with him expected, and on the way they were to fight many battles that would have turned back less ambitious men.

Though the land through which Cortes was to pass from the coast of Mexico to the interior is mountainous and mostly arid, he discovered a benign climate and generous valleys. The view below is the valley of Cuernavaca at the point from which Cortes first saw it in 1521.

III

WARRIORS AND ALLIES

An Aztec warrior with a feathered headdress holds a wicker shield in his left hand and a spear thrower called an atlatl in his right hand.

On August 31, the small Spanish column crossed the frontier of Tlaxcala, a state constantly at war with those parts of Mexico directly controlled by Montezuma. The Tlaxcalans recognized the power of the Aztecs but for generations had resolutely maintained their independence. There were other routes open to the Spanish conquistadors, but since Cortes did not want to leave a possible enemy at his rear as he went inland, he decided to attempt an alliance with the Tlaxcalans. He paused at the first town he came to and sent messengers forward with a scroll stating that he came in peace. But the messengers were treated as captives rather than envoys; one of them returned with the grim report that the Tlaxcalans intended to capture the Spaniards and sacrifice them to the god of war.

Once Cortes realized he had no recourse but battle, he commended himself and his men to God, unfurled his banners, and proceeded into Tlaxcala. The first day's march brought only a minor skirmish in which one man and two horses were lost. But on the second day the Spaniards found their way blocked by two armies of thousands of native warriors. For a brief time the forces faced each other while Cortes again explained that peaceful passage through the country was his only purpose. But, seeing the Tlaxcalans girding for the attack despite his pleas, Cortes raised his sword, and at once the battle was joined.

For a time it looked as if the Spaniards had at last met warriors who were their equal. And to make the fighting more evenly balanced, the terrain was so broken that the Spaniards' horses could not be brought into the fray. Finally, Cortes' men fought their way to level ground. There the cavalry came thundering to their assistance, and the cannon were unlimbered. The Spanish gunners fired round upon round into the mass of Indians, whose numbers were so great that even as they were slaughtered they almost overwhelmed the invaders. However, Cortes and his

Carved from black volcanic rock, the grimacing Aztec officer above is shown wearing an eagle-head helmet—which was an emblem of his knightly order.

men were fighting to survive, and the crossbows, guns, and steel began to tell against the natives' wooden spears and swords; fighting valiantly on, the conquistadors found themselves in possession of the field, with eight of the Indian captains dead and their warriors scattered.

When Cortes at last had time to savor the victory, he and his men thanked God and counted their wounded and dead. This was September 2, and they had traveled but a few miles on their march into Mexico toward a meeting with Montezuma.

They spent the next day resting, repairing their equipment, and making darts for the crossbows. Then they went out to count the enemy bodies, but they found none—the Tlaxcalans had taken their dead and wounded with them. This custom, which puzzled the Spaniards, was later discovered to be part of the natives' religious practices. It was necessary for the bodies of the dead to be dressed in the richest attire possible in order to be prepared for the after life in which the Indians believed. Thus the Spaniards had no idea how many men they had killed; nor did they know

The sketch of a Tlaxcalan village below was made by a scribe in 1581 in obedience to the Spanish king's command that a pictorial census be drafted. The location of each public building, house, and well in the village of Xonotla is shown; the native artist also tried, without much success, to show the relative elevation of the sites of the houses.

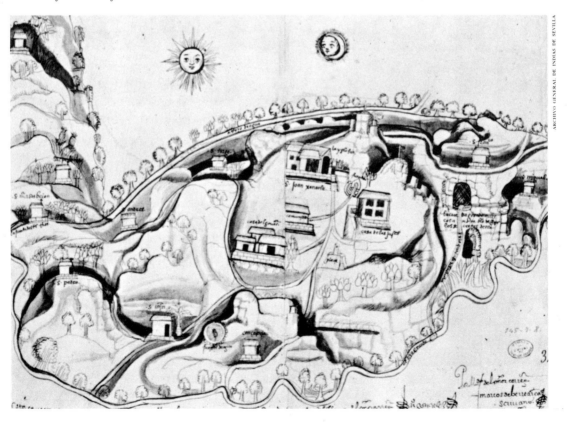

how many more warriors the Tlaxcalans could put into the field. The natives that were captured and then interrogated by Aguilar and Doña Marina reported that the Tlaxcalans were amassing an army numbered at fifty thousand: five great chiefs with ten thousand men each. Against them Cortes could now muster no more than four hundred men.

The Spaniards spent the night at confession, and the next morning they prepared to march forward once more. Even those who had been wounded picked themselves up off the ground, took their swords or lances in hand, and joined their companions. If this was going to be their last battle, they would all fight it together. Cortes advised the crossbowmen to be sparing of their darts and to take turns firing. He gave the same advice to the gunners. Then he named four men to guard his standard-bearer and gave the order to march forward to meet the enemy. Ahead, from the distant fields, they could hear the sound of drums and horns. The hillsides swarmed with Tlaxcalans and their allies. As Cortes and his soldiers neared the enemy lines, they could see among the ordinary warriors the brilliant colors of the feathered mantles and painted headdresses worn by the officers and chieftains. And above them all waved the banners of the great Tlaxcalan families.

A mighty war cry rose as the two forces rushed head-long at each other. The enemy filled the air with lances and arrows while the Spaniards held their fire until their cannon and guns could reach the center of the Indian masses. As Cortes' soldiers began blasting away at the enemy, every cannon shot and gunshot, every crossbow dart, and every sword found a target.

Nothing helped Cortes and his men more, however, than the dissension in the enemy ranks. The senior Indian captains would not cooperate with each other. Those who had committed their warriors to battle found that when they called for reinforcements, other war captains refused to move up their troops. And to the Indian foot soldiers, the Spanish steel was indeed terrifying. So too were the large snorting horses, which could trample a man to death. For all their numbers, the Indians of Tlaxcala were divided and frightened.

After the initial clash, the Indians fell back. This time they held their ranks in good order as they retreated, and though the Spanish horsemen tried to pursue, they were too weary to sit their horses. They reined in and turned back to their companions.

Fortunately, Cortes lost only a few men, but sixty had

In this eighteenth-century print the Tlaxcalan caciques listen to returned warriors who had been captured by Cortes but then released so they could carry his proposals for peace back to Tlaxcala. One of the men brandishes an atlatl.

been wounded, as well as all the horses. He buried his dead in secret and hid the graves, hoping to conceal from the superstitious Indians the fact that he and his soldiers were mortal. Then, after doctoring their wounds with the fat of dead Indians, his men rested. They were so tired they hardly noticed the height of the plain they had reached or the wind sweeping off the snow-covered mountains.

Once more Cortes tried to convince the Tlaxcalans that he did not want to fight. He sent messages to them repeating his first proposal: his only desire was to pass through their land on his way to visit Montezuma. As a further gesture of peace, he released the Tlaxcalan captains he had captured and sent them as messengers. Instead of listening to the renewed offer of peace, the Tlaxcalans listened to their priests, who told them that the Spaniards derived their strength from the sun. It was therefore decided that the invaders could be defeated in the darkness when the source of their strength had left them.

After sundown the Tlaxcalans prepared for a third assault on the invaders. Their war chief selected ten thousand of his bravest warriors and moved on the Spanish camp from three sides. Their plan had been kept secret, but in the bright moonlight that flooded the plain they could not move without casting long tell-tale shadows, and soon the Spanish sentries were alerted. Immediately Cortes prepared himself for the Indians' attack, but instead of waiting for the enemy to reach his camp, he sprang at them when they were still straggling into position. Into the bright night the Spanish horsemen charged, looming in the eyes of the panic-stricken Tlaxcalans like black apparitions. The Indians fought but briefly before breaking into flight, running vainly before the Spanish cavalrymen who rode them down and slaughtered them by the hundreds. For the Tlaxcalans it was a night of total defeat.

Yet even after three overwhelming defeats, the spirit of the Indians did not appear to be broken.

The troops of Cortes were, on the other hand, dispirited and exhausted by battle. The captain general now had fewer than 350 men, most of them wounded and ill. He himself was sick with fever. There was no word from his base at Villa Rica de Vera Cruz, and the Tlaxcalans still blocked the road westward.

If ever Cortes had reason to abandon his conquest, it was now. Instead, with his last grain of patience he tried to reason with the Tlaxcalans. Aguilar and Doña Marina attempted once more to convince the prisoners that Cortes meant their people no harm. Then he sent the prisoners home with a warning: there would either be peace in two days or the Spaniards would march on Tlaxcala, the Indians' capital, and kill them all. Cortes' men were not at all convinced that they could fulfill this threat, but they had reached such a state of despair that it no longer mattered very much. If called upon, they would do what they could.

The Tlaxcalan caciques were in council when the message from Cortes arrived. They carefully weighed the idea of a peaceful settlement. It was not a simple decision for them; it meant that they would have to accept their nation's defeat and face years, perhaps generations, of subjugation by the conquistadors. Finally, they conceded. They ordered their armies to withhold further attacks on the invaders. Then, to their surprise, the war chief rejected the plan. He would not admit that the Spanish soldiers could win, and even though many of his captains refused to fight a fourth time, the war chief called for an attack.

For several days Cortes awaited some word telling him

For defensive armor, both the Aztecs and the Tlaxcalans used shields of wicker covered with hides and painted with bright designs (above). As body protection they wore padded cotton suits soaked in brine and occasionally covered with feathers (at top). These were recognized by the Spaniards as both cooler and lighter than their steel armor and nearly as effective against arrows.

that he and his men would not have to face another battle. The unity of purpose among Cortes' men threatened to disintegrate—for the first time since he had scuttled his fleet at Villa Rica de Vera Cruz, there was murmuring dissension among his soldiers. Those who had objected to the campaign in the first place now repeated that they wanted to return to the coast and from there sail for Cuba. Cortes talked quietly to all of his men; he cajoled and made promises. He reminded them of the wealth they had seen and the fortunes that they would find ahead of them. For the moment they agreed to follow him.

At last a delegation from the Tlaxcalans arrived at the Spanish camp. But Cortes very soon discovered that what appeared to be a peace mission was in fact a spying mission. Infuriated, Cortes sent the spies back to the war chief after cutting off their hands, and with this gesture of finality, Cortes gave up all appearances of patience. The war faction, finally aware of the futility of further opposition to the Spaniards, gave up the fight. Soon, the Tlaxcalans came with their caciques and priests. They brought loads of food and gifts to the Spaniards and declared that they were ready to make peace. They kissed the earth at Cortes' feet and swore they would be his friends. The way was now clear through Tlaxcala, and the Spaniards had new allies to help them.

When news of the most recent Spanish alliance reached Montezuma, he once more sent his ambassadors to Cortes. This time the gifts they bore were larger, and in addition they told Cortes that their master, the great Emperor Montezuma, had offered to pay an annual tribute to King Charles and to Cortes himself. Montezuma demanded one condition: Cortes must stop his march and turn back to the coast. The Spanish victories against overwhelming odds confirmed Montezuma's fearful suspicions. He saw Cortes and his men as superhumans who had come to take over his realm.

Though Montezuma's policy was to stop Cortes by offering rich gifts and promising greater ones, his emissaries came to realize that the only plan Cortes had was a march through Mexico. They asked him if he would wait until they could send messengers for further orders from Montezuma before resuming his march. Cortes agreed. He was not well, nor were his men, and he needed time for his troops to recuperate and for his supplies to be replenished. At the end of six days an answer came from Montezuma: he sent gifts but no invitation to proceed into Mexico.

Unperturbed, Cortes began his journey westward, first stopping at the capital of Tlaxcala, which he and his men entered on September 23, twenty-four days and three battles after they had entered the land. Among the Tlaxcalans, Cortes was received with wild jubilation. He and his captains were feted at sumptuous banquets, and the caciques offered to give the Spaniards their daughters in marriage. Once the Spaniards had been assigned quarters and were made comfortable in the town, Cortes tried to find out as much as he could about the distant city where the Emperor Montezuma resided and about the Aztec people who dominated the interior of Mexico.

The caciques of Tlaxcala warned Cortes that Montezuma could put 150,000 warriors into the field any time he wished. They told him that the emperor ruled from a large city called Tenochtitlán, which was surrounded by a great salt lake. The Tlaxcalans explained how he extracted heavy taxes in the form of gold, silver, feathers, and precious jewels, and how he demanded that large numbers of men

As Doña Marina translates, Cortes grasps the hand of the Tlaxcalan cacique Xicoténcatl and settles peace terms. The Tlaxcalans, who had fought and lost four battles with the Spaniards, would prove their staunchest allies.

51

Among the many rich gifts given by Montezuma to Cortes is this mask of the chief Aztec god, Tezcatlipoca. It was made by covering a human skull with jewels and shells.

and women be sent to his capital as sacrifices to his gods. Cortes and his captains listened with awe—this was a land worth conquering.

The Tlaxcalans, who hated and feared the emperor and his people, tried to dissuade the Spaniards from continuing the foolhardy assault. Then suddenly, new emissaries arrived from Montezuma with an invitation for Cortes to visit him. The invitation was as surprising as it was courteous. Perhaps it was merely an attempt to lure the Spaniards farther into Mexico before overwhelming them; perhaps it was a device to separate the conquistadors from their new allies. As his men debated the reason for the emperor's change of heart, Cortes decided to march on to Tenochtitlán.

The Tlaxcalan caciques counseled him against trusting the Indians whom he would meet next, the Cholulans. Well known among surrounding tribes for their treachery, the Cholulans might be plotting—as a demonstration of their loyalty to Montezuma—to ensnare the Spanish forces. Cortes listened to the caciques and thanked them for their warning, but he indicated that he would still go to the Cholulans to arrange for a safe passage through their territory. He was determined to go cautiously and with the appearance of an explorer rather than a conqueror; so when the Tlaxcalans offered 10,000 men, he accepted only 1,000 to help carry supplies.

When the force was readied, Cortes, his soldiers, and his allies marched out of Tlaxcala down the broad road that led southwestward toward Cholula. The column of men and supplies was longer than when it had first left Villa Rica de Vera Cruz, and longer still than when it had left Cempoala. The Spaniards had fought hard and suffered losses, but in spite of bitter battles they had won allies.

After a short and uneventful march, the conquistadors arrived at the gates of the beautiful capital of the Cholulans. Here they were welcomed by the tribal leaders, who formed a public procession and led Cortes and his entourage through the crowd-lined streets to their quarters. They were housed in large villas and shown every sign of courtesy and hospitality.

Then the entire atmosphere changed. The caciques of Cholula refused to meet with the Spaniards. The steady supply of food dwindled and then stopped. When Cortes and his men tried to talk with the natives, they held their distance and laughed at the intruders.

Eventually a meeting with the Cholulan caciques was

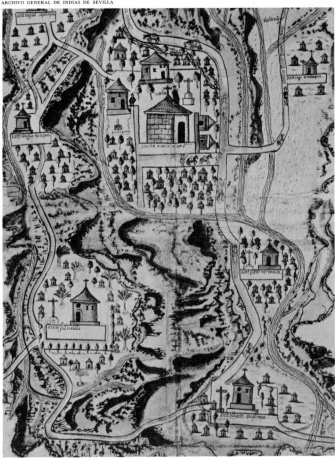

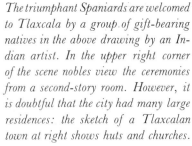

The triumphant Spaniards are welcomed to Tlaxcala by a group of gift-bearing natives in the above drawing by an Indian artist. In the upper right corner of the scene nobles view the ceremonies from a second-story room. However, it is doubtful that the city had many large residences: the sketch of a Tlaxcalan town at right shows huts and churches.

arranged. But meanwhile Cortes was told by his Cempoalan allies that holes with stakes set in them to impale the Spaniards' horses were being dug in the streets and camouflaged. And from the Tlaxcalans he learned that the Cholulans had made sacrifices for battle the night before and that they were moving their women and children into the hills beyond the city.

Further confirmation of a plot against the Spaniards was discovered by Doña Marina. The wife of a cacique, an old woman who admired Doña Marina, approached the interpreter and suggested that she flee because the Spaniards would be ambushed on the next day as they left the city. Doña Marina listened to the old woman and learned that Montezuma had sent presents to the Cholulan war captains and had asked them to capture the strangers and bring them to his capital. Satisfied that she knew the entire plan, Doña Marina agreed to leave the city with the old

TEXT CONTINUED ON PAGE 56

This shocking water color of the massacre at Cholula was painted as an illustration for the works of Bartolmé de las Casas, a priest who hoped to dissuade the Spaniards from future cruelty to the Indians. Men and women of Cholula are shown being beaten and put to the sword as they try to carry the Spaniards' heavy baggage.

TEXT CONTINUED FROM PAGE 53

woman, but first she asked permission to collect her belongings. Doña Marina rushed back and reported the conversation to Cortes, who ordered the old woman to be taken into custody so that the Cholulans would not know that he had learned their plans.

He quickly called a meeting of his captains to decide what steps to take. An escape from the city would be impossible because the Spaniards were hemmed in by the city walls. And a pitched battle within the city would be risky because there was little room for the cavalry to maneuver. Nevertheless, they would be fighting when and where they chose, and they would have the advantage of surprising the Cholulans. A long and watchful night began.

The next morning the area surrounding the buildings that housed the Spaniards was swarming with warriors. Instead of sending the carriers for which Cortes had asked in his negotiations, the caciques had sent troops posing as carriers. They pressed into the small plaza and overflowed the streets beyond. Out of the mass of Indians Cortes called the caciques aside, informed them that he knew about the plot against him, and formally accused them of treachery. The Cholulan caciques were aghast; they wondered if the Spaniards were able to read their minds, and immediately they tried to throw the blame for their actions on Montezuma. But Cortes hardly listened. Confident in the readiness of his forces, and determined to press for battle, he gave the signal.

A gunshot broke over the crowded plaza. The Cholulan warriors, trapped between the walls and the Spanish horsemen, were stunned by the fury of the assault. Barely able to defend themselves, they fell before the Spanish onslaught like harvested grain.

After almost two hours of brutal killing, Cortes' Tlaxcalan allies, who had been outside of the city, joined in the melee and plundered the town. All through that day and night and into the next day, the Tlaxcalans ran wild through the city, killing, stealing, and destroying.

A pall settled over Cholula. Scores of dead lay in the streets. Many of the houses had been destroyed. Cholula was its own grave; six thousand or more Indians had been killed. The massacre was so complete that some historians have concluded that Cortes intended it to be a warning to the Mexicans.

Then the men from the neighboring towns came forward to meet with Cortes. They contended that the Cholulans had only planned what had been ordered by the

Sixteenth-century Spanish officers and courtiers prized the supple and decorative swords made in Italy. This slender Spanish sword of Italian make is dated about 1560.

METROPOLITAN MUSEUM OF ART, ROGERS FUND, 1904

56

emperor; they wanted to be forgiven, and they begged to have their nation pardoned.

Cortes could afford to be kind now, and he readily agreed to pardon them so long as they knew what would happen if they ever tried treachery again. Aware that the ambassadors of Montezuma were listening to him as well, he said also that he would forgive the Cholulans because of his high regard for Montezuma, whose subjects they were. He did not as yet want to give up the pretense that Montezuma was his friend and that the Spaniards came in peace.

After this diplomatic ceremony, Cortes ordered the Tlaxcalans to release the Cholulan prisoners they had taken, and then he began to make peace between the two nations, hoping to solidify the alliance of Spaniards and Indians.

Word of this newest Spanish victory and the resulting alliances spread throughout Mexico. Rumor and fact combined to create the belief among the natives that the Spaniards were invincible.

Cortes remained in Cholula for several weeks, parleying with the emissaries of Montezuma and preparing to march to the city on the lake. Rumors reached him that Montezuma was conferring with his priests about what he should do. Cortes heard too that the answer Montezuma

At left is one part of a long roll of canvas painted by the Tlaxcalans to record scenes of the Spanish conquest. This section shows the Tlaxcalans finishing off Cholulans penned in an enclosure while Cortes and Doña Marina watch. The canvas was made for King Charles as a reminder of the faithful service of his Tlaxcalan allies.

received from his holy men was to allow the Spaniards to enter his city and then destroy them at his leisure.

Knowing what he and his men would be marching into, Cortes consulted his captains. All of them agreed: they would proceed into Mexico as planned. With four thousand Indian bearers, the conquistadors marched out of Cholula toward Montezuma's capital.

They had not gone very far when they were met once again by the emperor's ambassadors. This time Montezuma wanted Cortes to know he was to come no closer to

With a religious banner streaming behind them, Cortes and Doña Marina (far right in the scene below) set out for Mexico City. At left, in a detail from a 1585 chronicle, Montezuma ponders whether to flee (top) or hide in a cave (bottom).

the capital. If the Spaniards would give up the march, a great tribute would be paid in gold and silver. The ambassadors listed their new reasons: the road was narrow; there was not enough food for the Spaniards and their Indian allies; and Montezuma's vassal states were protesting the entrance of the invaders into the country. Cortes and his officers replied that they understood what had been said to them, but that they had come too far to turn back now. Disregarding further protests from the ambassadors, they continued their march. As the Mexicans were to say in later years, "They hungered after gold like pigs."

In their quest for gold, and for the ruler who controlled its steady flow into the Aztec treasuries, the conquistadors had indeed marched far—some 275 miles over mountainous country to the great Valley of Mexico. As they continued down the eastward slopes of the valley, they entered the strange, lake-bound world where the Aztecs had settled and prospered in the two centuries immediately preceding Cortes' arrival.

The four large lakes on which the Aztec cities had been built actually comprised one vast inland salt sea (see map on page 116). The capital, Tenochtitlán, stood on an island off the west shore of the largest lake, Lake Texcoco. Passage to or from the city could only be made by means of one of three major causeways—from the north, south, or west. These broad roads, made of stone and rubble, were vital to the supplying and defense of the city, as any visitor could tell at a glance (see endsheets).

Whether Cortes had been informed of the city's strategic location by his allies, or whether he had formed any military plan, is unknown. He seems merely to have relied on the reputation that preceded him and on the might of his arms. But as he and his men descended to the waters of the first lake, Lake Chalco, they must have stared into the hazy distance and wondered whether massed armies or an imperial procession would be waiting to greet them.

Then one morning a great causeway appeared in the distance. Spreading before them was the broad avenue leading toward Montezuma's capital. Years later Bernal Díaz del Castillo wrote: "We saw so many cities and villages built in the water and other great towns on dry land, and that straight and level causeway going toward Mexico, we were amazed . . . and some of our soldiers even asked whether the things that we saw were not a dream. [We were] seeing things . . . that had never been heard of or seen before, not even dreamed about."

Cortes (under the number 18 at left) rides to his meeting with Monte-zuma (crowned, at right), unaware that many Aztecs believed him to be the white god Quetzalcoatl, whose return had been foretold in legend.

60

IV

THE CITY
IN THE LAKE

Riding at the head of his column, Cortes approached the city of Tenochtitlán from the south. As his eye swept over the vast, towered city, the nearest structure to impress him was a fortified gate standing at the head of the causeway over which he would have to pass. As he began his march on to the long causeway, the gate suddenly opened and a procession of well-dressed Mexicans came forth to greet him. When they stood just a few paces from him, they knelt down, and each put one hand on the ground and then kissed the earth.

When these preliminaries were completed, Cortes signaled for his men to move on. The Spanish soldiers noted that the great causeway over which they were marching was bridged in several places so that water could run beneath. These large wooden bridges were removable, leaving gaps that could block any entrance or exit from the city. As the Spaniards filed on toward the city, they realized that they might be entering a trap from which there was little chance of escape.

Then as they crossed over one of the largest bridges, Emperor Montezuma appeared with his personal retinue. Cortes described the meeting in a letter to King Charles:

We were received by Montezuma with about two hundred chiefs, all barefooted and dressed in a kind of very rich livery. They approached in two processions along the walls of the street, which is very broad and straight and very beautiful. Montezuma came in the middle of the street with two lords, one on each side of him. . . . All were dressed in the same manner except that Montezuma was shod and the other lords were barefooted. As we approached each other I descended from my horse and was about to embrace him, but the two lords in attendance intervened so that I should not touch him, and then they, and he also, made the ceremony of kissing the ground. Having done this, he or-

Two of the most important Aztec deities were the peace-loving Quetzalcoatl, god of civilization (below at right), and the warlike Huitzilopochtli (above), who ordered the Aztecs to found Tenochtitlán.

dered his brother to take me by the arm, and the other attendant walked a little ahead of us. After he spoke to me, all the other lords who formed the two processions saluted me one after the other and then returned to the procession. As I approached to speak to Montezuma, I took off a collar of pearls and glass diamonds that I wore and put it on his neck. After we had gone through some of the streets, one of his servants came with two collars which were made of colored shells. From each of the collars hung eight golden shrimps executed with great perfection and a span long. He took the collars from the servant and put them on my neck, and we continued on through the streets until we came to a large and handsome house, which he had prepared for our reception.

The scene that Cortes described so vividly—the arrival of the Spanish invaders in the Mexican capital—took place on November 8, 1519. Although the construction of this great city had been begun by the Aztecs less than two centuries before, the roots from which the Aztec civilization had grown were ancient. The dress and manners and buildings that Cortes now observed were the culmination of many thousands of years of cultural development in the fertile valleys of the central Mexican highlands.

The archaeological record of the Aztecs' ancestors goes back to nomadic hunters who some eight thousand years ago stalked the mammoth and other prehistoric creatures that roamed through the shallow lakes of Central America. Much later, about 2000 B.C., these nomads began to settle down and establish villages in what is now Mexico. They learned to make weapons, tools, and pottery. Slowly, small communities began to group together under the leadership of chiefs and priests; people learned to share information and resources. Finally, sometime around the birth of Christ, their efforts crystallized into a distinct and unique cultural pattern.

This peak of early Indian development in Mexico has its own memorial—the great archaeological site of Teotihuacán just north of Mexico City. No written records of the classic civilization of Teotihuacán survive, but these magnificent ruins indicate that the site was contemporary with the great period of the Maya. And like the brilliant Mayan cities, Teotihuacán also went into eclipse. There

On this Indian map, made for the Spanish viceroy Antonio de Mendoza in 1541, the city of Tenochtitlán appears symbolically as an eagle perched on a cactus. Such an omen had told the Aztecs where to locate their capital.

arose from its ruins, however, two great empires. The first of these was that of the Toltecs, who fought their way to dominance in central Mexico and ruled much of the region for several hundred years. The second empire was that of the Mexica, which came to be known as the Aztec nation. All across Mexico in postclassic times, the competition for land and power among various Indian city-states was tremendous, and those who gained control did so through their military prowess.

The legendary history of the Aztecs, often retold by the people around their hearths, symbolized this rise to military dominance. The Aztecs came into the Valley of Mexico as a savage but ambitious people following the dictates of their god Huitzilopochtli. He and other chief deities were gods of war who demanded countless numbers of human sacrifices, and for that purpose rather than for territorial gain, their worshipers were aroused to become warriors and conquerors.

After many years as barbaric wanderers, the Aztecs were given a heavenly sign, as they had expected. For it had been foretold that at some time during their wanderings an eagle with a snake in its mouth would be seen perched on a cactus. Following the legend, the Aztecs founded a city where an eagle appeared, naming the spot Tenochtitlán. Through unfaltering adherence to the wishes

The Teotihuacán culture flourished in Mexico long before the arrival of the Aztecs. The huge Pyramid of the Sun (left), over 200 feet high, was erected around A.D. 100, in the first Teotihuacán period.

of the gods, and by their personal valor, they conquered the original inhabitants, overcame neighboring tribes, and became the dominant people of Mexico.

The Aztecs, impressed by the wealth and culture of some of the tribes they conquered, labored to perfect their own state. By the time of Cortes' arrival, their achievements had equaled and in some cases surpassed all other Indian civilizations of the New World. In the realm of government the Aztecs developed their own system of tribunals to administer justice; they had their own viceroys to rule their provinces, which spread across the land from the Atlantic to the Pacific; and to communicate between their states they set up a messenger service as efficient as any in Europe. In science they had knowledge of medicine and had begun to experiment with herbs, classifying them along with the diseases they cured. In art their architecture was impressive, and their sculpture brilliant. And of all their accomplishments, the art of war was the one the Aztecs had developed most highly. Their aptitude for military matters and their emphasis on training and discipline impressed the Spanish conquistadors and was even respected by them.

It was with the leader of these skillful and dedicated barbarians that Cortes entered Tenochtitlán, and in the months that followed, the two leaders came to know each other fairly intimately. To Cortes, Montezuma seemed to be all powerful, yet at the same time curiously weak—confused and indecisive as to how he should cope with the intruders. At one moment Montezuma appeared ready to resist the Spanish invasion and at another time almost to welcome it. Only later did the Spaniards learn a possible explanation for the Aztec emperor's hesitancy: once he had been a renowned warrior, so successful that in one campaign he had rounded up thousands of sacrificial captives; then he had taken on priestly duties, and in that role he was less sure, uncertain whether to obey the dictates of the Aztecs' many gods or his own strong intelligence and will.

But there was yet another reason for Montezuma's apparent confusion. It was because of the legend of the Aztecs' great god Quetzalcoatl, who was supposed to return one day to revisit his people.

Quetzalcoatl, according to legend, was a hero who had been the human leader of the ancient Toltecs as well as an immortal deity. He was fair and bearded, and he taught his obedient people many things—how to plant, how to work metal, and how to construct beautiful buildings. But

The Temple of Quetzalcoatl at Teotihuacán was erected around A.D. 250, during the second Teotihuacán period, and is ornamented with heads of the Feathered Serpent, one of the god's many symbols.

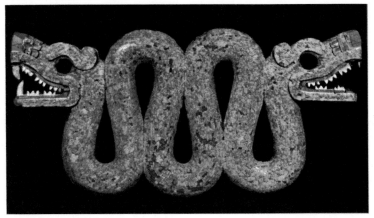

Religion played a vital part in all aspects of Aztec life. This turquoise and shell breast ornament is shaped into the form of a double-headed serpent and probably symbolized the Aztecs' belief in the continuity and duality of life.

Quetzalcoatl was driven out by a rival, a king and deity named Tezcatlipoca. And after a long period of wandering, Quetzalcoatl disappeared across the eastern sea, promising to return in the year *ce acatl* (one reed)—which in the Aztec calendar is the name of a certain year that recurs every fifty-two years.

To Montezuma and his priests it seemed more than mere chance that a white-skinned man had landed on the coast of Mexico and begun a march inland in the year *ce acatl*. These legends were real and holy to the Aztecs, as important as the Gospels were to the Spaniards. And so, torn between his dread of the invader who was causing his subject states to rebel against him and his fears that this invader might be Quetzalcoatl, Montezuma hesitated and could not act.

He was indeed a complex man, intelligent and impressive in appearance. Bernal Díaz del Castillo wrote:

The Great Montezuma was about forty years old, of good height and well proportioned, slender and spare of flesh . . . He did not wear his hair long, but so as to cover his ears; his scanty beard was well shaped and thin. His face was somewhat long, but cheerful, and he had good eyes and showed in his appearance and manner both tenderness and, when necessary, gravity. He was very neat and clean . . .

Making every effort to be gracious to his unwelcome guests, Montezuma put at the disposal of Cortes and his companions a large palace with a center courtyard. Here the Spaniards bedded down in adequate, if not sumptuous, comfort. For several days they remained close to their quarters. Then Cortes sent Doña Marina with a message telling Montezuma that he would like to meet him at the

The Aztecs worshiped the forces of nature through a multitude of gods, each with his appropriate title and symbol. The three great gods were Quetzalcoatl, the Feathered Serpent; Huitzilopochtli, the war god, whose symbol was the humming bird; and Tezcatlipoca, chief of the gods, who was called Smoking Mirror after the device used by the Aztecs to kindle their ritual fires. Other important gods were those of agriculture and fertility: Tlaloc, the rain god; Centeol, the corn god; Ehecatl, the wind god, whose mask of mosaic-covered wood is at left; Xipe, the Flayed One, god of seedtime and planting, whose priest wore a flayed human skin as a costume in imitation of the god.

67

great temple, or *teocalli*, where the Aztecs worshiped Huitzilopochtli. As always, Montezuma hesitated before he finally agreed.

Taking almost all of his men and horses, Cortes rode out to meet his host at the great temple. When the Spaniards arrived, Montezuma was at the top of the temple making human sacrifices. Several Aztecs came forward to help Cortes to the top, but the Spanish captain general brushed them aside and mounted the 114 steps unaided. At the top of the temple, Cortes and his companions were horrified to find the Aztec idols spattered with flesh and blood. The whole place reeked, and on the floor there was more blood, encrusted and black. Shocked and repelled by what he saw, Cortes tried to explain to the emperor-priest that these idols were no more than devils and that the sacrifice of humans was blasphemous. The mighty Aztec, injured by the Spaniard's remarks, said that his gods were good and that he regretted having allowed the Spaniards to visit the temple at all. Seeing that his host was angry, Cortes quickly made overtures to pacify the emperor and then departed.

The illustration below from the official Spanish history of their conquest shows the huge Aztec temple at Tenochtitlán. Wide stairs lead to the sacrificial platform where Cortes attempted to stop Montezuma from making a human sacrifice.

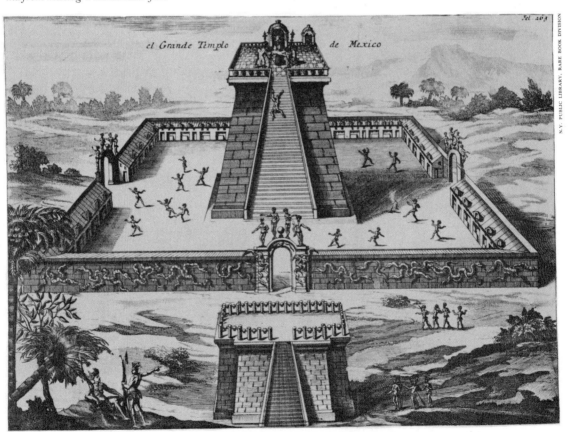

The bloodthirsty war god Huitzilo-pochtli demanded the sacrifice of a living human's heart. The Indian drawing at right pictures an Aztec priest performing the gruesome rite on a temple roof as another victim lies at the foot of the steps. The Aztecs raided their neighbors for victims because captured warriors made the most desirable offerings. As these raids spread they became a campaign of conquest and led at last to the formation of an empire.

As Cortes turned to descend the steps of the high temple, a view of the great city spread out before him. He described it in a letter to his king:

This great city is built on a salt lake, and from the mainland to the city is a distance of two leagues from any side from which you enter. It has four approaches by means of artificial cause-ways, two cavalry lances in width. The city is as large as Seville or Córdoba. The principal streets are very broad and well-constructed. Over them ten horsemen can ride abreast. . . .

Cortes returned directly to his quarters and called his captains together. They agreed that they had to do something to make themselves more secure from possible attack. At length they developed a desperate plan but hesitated to use it. The next morning Cortes was still undecided when news arrived from the coast that forced him to act. Two of his Tlaxcalan allies entered Tenochtitlán with word that the Aztecs had attacked Villa Rica de Vera Cruz, killing seven Spanish soldiers. In addition, the neighboring townspeople were in revolt against the Spaniards and had refused to supply them with food. This was the first Spanish disaster, and Cortes knew there would be more unless he acted quickly.

Calling five of his captains together—Pedro de Alvarado, Gonzalo de Sandoval, Juan Velásquez de Leon, Francisco de Lugo, and Alonzo de Avila—as well as Bernal Díaz del Castillo—Cortes told them to arm themselves and join him. Then he sent a message to Montezuma informing the emperor that he was coming to visit the royal palace.

69

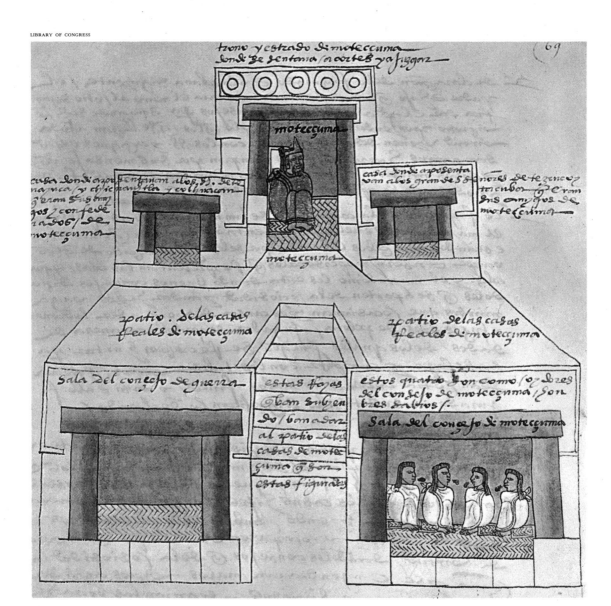

trono y estzado de moteccuma
dond ze zentaua sor cortes y a siggoz

(69)

moteccuma

moteccuma

casa dond aposentauan alos ss. seta-
naçca y chiemantla y colhuacan
geron sus bua-
gos y confede
rados/ se
moteccuma

casa dond aposenta
uan alos grandes ss. nozes de tezcuco y
tacubor q eron
ans amygos de
moteccuma

patio. delas casas
seales de moteccuma

patio delas casas
seales de moteccuma

sala del conçeso de guerra

estas tazas
sstan subsen
do/ son adexo
al patio dela
casas de mote
çuma q son
estas figuras

estos quatro son como oydozes
del conçeso de moteccuma son
tzes saltos/

sala del conçeso de moteccuma

When Cortes and his captains stood before the Aztec ruler, Cortes described the critical situation on the coast and accused Montezuma of having brought it about—a charge which the emperor promptly denied. Cortes further told Montezuma that he wished him to return with the Spaniards to their quarters until the matter was cleared up. He promised that Montezuma would be well treated, with all the honor due an emperor, and that he should not consider himself a prisoner.

Shocked at the thought that anyone would try to abduct him while in his own palace, Montezuma told the Spaniard that no one had the right to order him about and that he would not leave with the Spaniards. Montezuma parleyed and argued. He even offered to give up a son and two daughters as hostages, but the Spaniards were in no mood to compromise. The tedious tugging and pulling finally caused the Spanish captains who were with Cortes to become restless and angry.

When Montezuma saw just how provoked the Spaniards were, he finally yielded. He called for his litter and told his attendants that he was joining Cortes and the Spanish force of his own free will.

With trusted captains stationed beside the litter to prevent the emperor from escaping, the small group marched back through the streets of Tenochtitlán to Cortes' quarters. From that moment on, Montezuma was at the complete mercy of the conquistadors. When instructed to order the Indian leaders who had attacked Villa Rica de Vera Cruz to be delivered up to Cortes, Montezuma had no choice: immediately he sent out orders for the men to be brought to the capital.

Installing Montezuma at Cortes' palace caused much consternation among the Indians, and rumors spread that the emperor had been carried away by force. Montezuma quieted the unrest by explaining that the decision to live with the Spaniards was his alone, and he warned his people to keep the peace. There was one small outbreak, but Montezuma himself ordered this stopped.

The caciques who had attacked the coastal base arrived and confessed that they had killed the Spaniards there.

In this sixteenth-century drawing, Montezuma suffers the indignity of being shackled by Cortes after being imprisoned in Cortes' palace.

Montezuma's palace (at left, above) contained the imperial apartments (top) with rooms for important chiefs on either side. On the ground floor were council chambers where the emperor's advisers can be seen in consultation. The flint-bladed knife at left, below was used in the bloody Aztec rites.

However, at the same time they confirmed that they had acted under orders from Montezuma. When Cortes faced the emperor with the charge, he again denied any responsibility for the incident. To keep peace between himself and the Aztec ruler, Cortes accepted the lie. He condemned the rebellious caciques to death, and to make it clear to all that the Spaniards were in power, he had the men burned at the stake before Montezuma's own palace.

Cortes knew this was a bold stroke and that it could quickly breed further violence against him. His only insurance was Montezuma, and so he ordered the emperor shackled during the executions. When there was no stir against Cortes' actions, he ordered the shackles removed and apologized to the emperor for having subjected him to this indignity.

All of the rest of the time that Montezuma remained a Spanish prisoner he was treated with great deference. The soldiers who came into his presence removed their helmets. He met with his counselors and family whenever he wished. The one time a soldier insulted the emperor, Cortes ordered the man punished.

In the weeks that followed, a strange friendship developed between the Aztec ruler and his captors. He learned to know each of those with whom he came in contact. He gave them presents of gold and silver, bolts of fine cloth,

The gold ornaments at left are the work of Mixtec craftsmen, contemporaries of the Aztecs, who were famous for their skill as goldsmiths. In the upper row are an owl's head, a lip plug in the form of a snake, and a ring decorated with a human head; in the lower, a monkey-head pendant, an ear plug, and the small figure of a god. At right is a ceremonial shield adorned with feather mosaic and outlined in gold leaf. Feathers were cut into small pieces and attached to a base material to form a picture. This type of decoration was widely used by the Aztecs.

and maidservants. At the same time, the Spaniards came to respect and admire Montezuma.

For a time it appeared as though the Spaniards had seized control of all Mexico by the simple tactic of holding the country's ruler a prisoner. Sandoval, the youngest of Cortes' trusted captains, was sent back to assume command at Villa Rica de Vera Cruz. From there he sent to Tenochtitlán the gear stripped from two of the vessels that had been scuttled before the long march inland, and Cortes, with the help of Montezuma, built two small ships for patrol work on Lake Texcoco.

Cortes and Montezuma used one of the ships for their hunting expeditions on the well-stocked royal game reservation across the lake. As the trust between the two men grew, Montezuma was allowed to visit his temple to worship, even though the Spaniards were opposed to the manner in which he did this. It seemed for a time as if the peace would last.

Cortes in his own way helped keep the countryside stirred up by demanding that all of the available gold in the area be brought to Tenochtitlán as tribute. With this tribute, and with other treasure that had belonged to

One of the most important sources of information on the Aztecs is a late sixteenth-century treatise written by the monk Bernardino de Sahagún and illustrated by native artists. Above at left, a farmer plants maize with a crude digging stick while at right two Aztecs gather and shuck the corn.

Montezuma's father, the Spaniards were kept busy for days
just assessing the value of their loot. The small pieces removed from Aztec jewelry alone was valued at 600,000
pesos. Goldsmiths were brought in from a nearby town,
and they smelted the gold into slabs. The Spaniards were
unable to weigh the treasure accurately, and Cortes suggested that no one take his share until it could be divided
more equitably. But the captains and the soldiers had come
too far and fought too hard to be put off. They demanded
a division of the spoils, and Cortes had to consent.

First, the "royal fifth" was removed. Then a portion
was set aside for those who had remained at Villa Rica de
Vera Cruz. There were ugly reports that a third of what
was left had been hidden for Cortes' own use, and some of
the captains appeared to be taking even more before the
general division was made. Finally, Cortes took the fifth
that was promised him when he had become captain general
at Villa Rica de Vera Cruz so many months before. Then
he demanded to be repaid from what was left for the money
he had spent in buying ships and supplying the expedition.
After that he asked that a share be put aside to pay Velásquez
for his ships, which had been destroyed. Then the priests

*Crouching over a fire, a goldsmith (above, left) casts an ornament by the
"lost wax" process: a wax model is covered in clay and baked until the wax
runs out, leaving a hollow into which molten gold is poured. At right two
feather-mosaic makers are at work. A finished jacket lies beside them.*

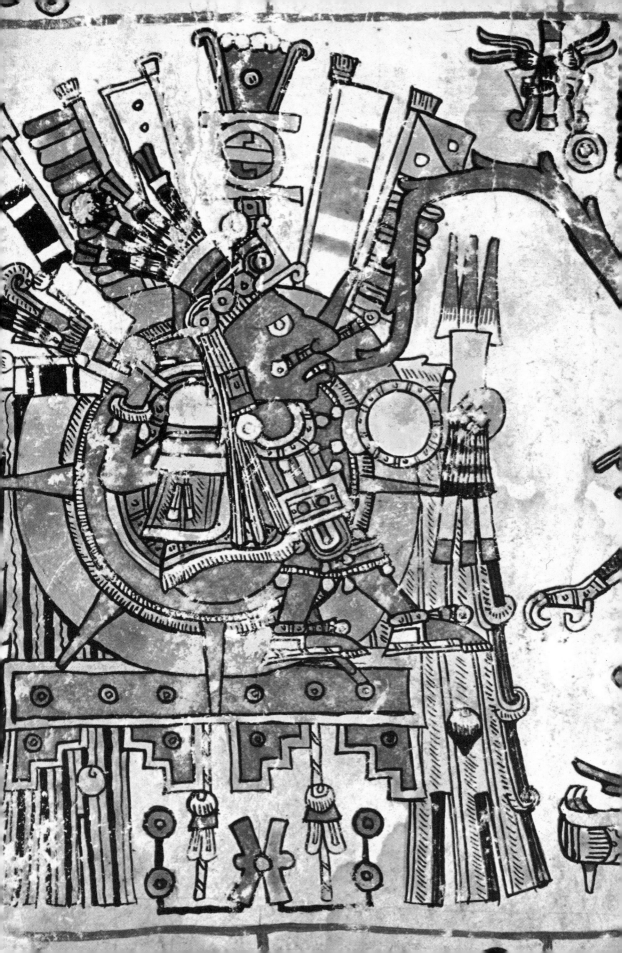

took their share, followed by the captains. Those who had brought horses took double shares. So did the crossbowmen and the gunners.

Finally, the common soldiers were told that they could divide what remained, but so little remained that many of them did not even bother to take their shares, and these also went to Cortes. There was grumbling, but none felt he could speak out and receive justice, and so the matter was settled by some flattering speeches Cortes made. The Spaniards who had suddenly become wealthy hoped for more still, and those who had failed to become rich had no choice but to hope for the future.

The one remaining concern of the Spaniards was the Aztecs' continuing custom of human sacrifice. Both the brutality and the blasphemy of this practice offended the Spanish priests and officers; they complained bitterly and frequently to Cortes. Finally, Cortes told Montezuma that he must abandon this practice. Montezuma, afraid of incurring the wrath of his gods, refused. But a compromise was reached: the Spaniards were given a place in the great temple to worship. Here they set up an image of the Virgin Mary and a cross, and they set a soldier to guard their shrine. Eventually they hoped to convert the emperor.

The compromise might have satisfied Montezuma temporarily, but not his followers. His priests reported that the Aztec gods wanted no part of the strange deity and wished to leave Mexico. They also complained that the gold used to honor their gods had been melted down to satisfy the invaders. The priests took their message to the people, and Tenochtitlán seethed with resentment against the small band of conquistadors who now held, in addition to the emperor, five of the principal caciques.

Montezuma, knowing the temper of his people, warned Cortes that there might be an attack upon the Spaniards. He was convinced that Cortes could only save his men by leaving the city immediately. The emperor repeated that this was the only way they could save their lives.

Cortes and his captains listened as Doña Marina interpreted. Then the captain general told the emperor that there were two problems facing him at this moment. One of them was that he could not withdraw his men from Mexico because he had no ships waiting for him on the

The Spanish horseman above bears a cross, which would be raised in a captured Aztec town by the monks who were with Cortes' expedition.

Many human victims were offered to the sun god, Tonatiuh (left), every year. These rites were viewed with horror by the Spaniards, who tried to end them.

77

In 1520 two challenges confronted Cortes. First, fierce Aztec warriors (right) clad in padded armor and armed with flint-tipped clubs stood between him and the sea. Second, Velasquez's fleet had arrived at Villa Rica de Vera Cruz. Cortes wrote to King Charles of his fears in a series of letters published in 1522. At left is an illustration from this edition showing Spanish troopships under full sail.

coast, and the other was that he would have to take Montezuma with him in the event he should leave.

Despondent at the prospect before him, Montezuma agreed to speak to his priests and chieftains to see if he could persuade them to postpone the attack. In this way Montezuma would allow the Spaniards time to send orders to the coast to begin immediately the construction of three sea-going vessels. Cortes thanked Montezuma for his help and rejoined the rest of his men.

The Spaniards of all ranks knew they were in great trouble. Doña Marina had heard enough in the town to believe that a major uprising was inevitable, and the Tlaxcalans who had come with Cortes reported the same news. A strong guard was placed around Montezuma because the captive emperor remained the only true security the Spaniards had. They slept in their armor, their equipment beside them, with their horses saddled and bridled.

It was now May of 1520; Cortes had been in Tenochtitlán since November, and he had only succeeded in trapping himself. He did not see how he could withdraw to a point of safety, and it did not appear that there was any way for him to stay where he was if the the city rose against him. Then suddenly he learned that he had other problems, equally pressing. A Spanish fleet sent from Cuba by Velásquez had landed at Villa Rica de Vera Cruz.

FROM SANTIAGO

In the year that had passed since the eleven ships of Cortes had set sail from Cuba, Governor Velásquez had grown increasingly anxious. Even before Cortes had cleared Cuba's shores, it was evident that the brash captain general had no intention of staying under the governor's thumb; now, in addition, Velásquez received word that Cortes had sent a treasure-laden ship to Spain and had then scuttled the remainder of his fleet. It was clear to the aged governor that the very man he had picked to head the expedition was now trying to set himself up on the mainland under the direct authority of the king. Swiftly, Velásquez took two steps to prevent this: he organized a new expedition to sail immediately for the mainland, and he sought diplomatic means to undercut any influence Cortes' representatives might find at the king's court.

At that moment King Charles was impatient with court matters and paper work because he was about to leave Spain for the Low Countries in order to consolidate his rule over those European states that comprised the Holy Roman Empire. Hence, Cortes' letter was placed in the hands of the Bishop of Burgos, Juan Rodriguez de Fonseca, president of the Royal Council of the Indies. It was to the bishop, a relative by marriage, that Velásquez appealed for help. Being more disposed to the cause of his kinsman, the bishop sent a hasty order to Velásquez that by any and all means he was to capture Cortes and his men.

This time Velásquez mounted an even larger fleet than he had assembled before. Over nine hundred soldiers were loaded aboard ships in Santiago harbor. They carried twenty cannon, eighty horses, and seventy gunners. The governor of Cuba wanted to be certain that Cortes and those who had sailed with him would be overwhelmed.

Tales of Velásquez's preparations reached the island of Santo Domingo where the court of Spain had established a

This illustration for the title page of an edition of Cortes' letters to King Charles shows the conqueror, surrounded by his captains, kneeling at right. Charles and his courtiers (left) wait to receive Cortes' petitions.

tribunal to oversee activities in all islands of the Carib-bean. The Royal Audience, as this tribunal was called, was very much concerned about peace in the area, and a repre-sentative, Lucas Vázquez de Ayllón, was sent to Cuba to stop the powerful fleet from sailing for Mexico. Although Ayllón threatened Velásquez with heavy fines if he sent Spaniard to fight Spaniard, the governor ignored the threat. He knew he had support at home in the Council of the In-dies, and that was more important. Unable to prevent its departure, Ayllón decided to sail with the fleet to see what he might be able to do on the mainland to prevent a bloody clash.

This time Velásquez picked a very different man to be his captain—Pánfilo de Narváez. A capable and seasoned veteran who had accompanied Velásquez in the conquest of Cuba, Narváez had been on the island almost as long as the governor himself. Under Narváez's command, the fleet sailed from Cuba for the mainland. On the fourth night out the sea grew rough. Several of the smaller vessels foundered and fifty men were drowned. The rest of the fleet continued on, and in mid-April, 1520, put in at San Juan de Ulúa, where Cortes had anchored thirteen months before. Here, Narváez had luck. Three scouts whom Cortes had sent out in search of gold and copper mines heard about the landing of a large fleet and managed to reach the camp of their countrymen. Narváez welcomed them and listened with delight as they told him everything he wanted to know about Cortes. The discontented trio also located Villa Rica de Vera Cruz on the map for Narváez and informed him that its undermanned garrison was commanded by the youthful Gonzalo de Sandoval.

Narváez listened to the three soldiers and made his plans to move on Villa Rica de Vera Cruz. In the mean-time, he made direct contact with Montezuma without Cortes' knowledge. Cortes had allowed the Aztec caciques free access to their emperor, and they had taken advantage of it. No sooner had the large fleet appeared off the main-land than Montezuma was informed. He secretly urged his caciques to aid the newcomers and to tell them that he was a prisoner of Cortes.

Word quickly came back from Narváez to Montezuma stating that Cortes and his men were renegades acting with-out the orders of their king and that he, Narváez, had been sent to punish Cortes and his men and at the same time set Montezuma free.

Delighted with what he heard, Montezuma studied the

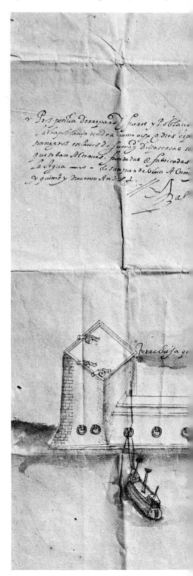

Cortes landed at the island of San Juan de Ulúa in 1519. By 1590, when the sketch below was made, the island was a thriving port with a church in the plaza (top) and sizable fortifications to defend the Spanish treasure fleet (bottom).

A contemporary Spaniard described Cuba's governor Diego Velásquez (far left) as "... covetous of glory, and somewhat more covetous of wealth." Though sly and powerful, he was unable to regain the loyalty of young cavaliers like Gonzalo de Sandoval, who had come to prominence under Cortes. In the eighteenth-century portrait at left, Sandoval wears a plumed helmet.

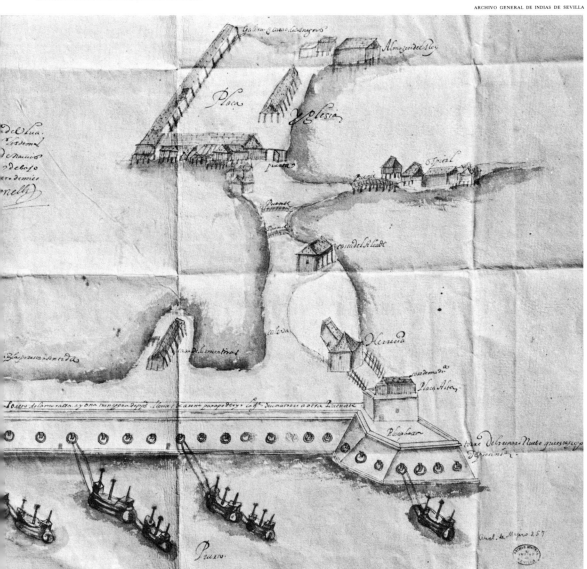

A memorable view of Cortes' departure from Tenochtitlán to challenge Narváez was presented by the great American historian William Prescott: "Montezuma in his royal litter, borne on the shoulders of his nobles and escorted by the Spanish infantry, accompanied the general to the causeway. There, embracing him in the most cordial manner, they parted. . . ." In the illustration of that scene at left, Cortes bids the Emperor Montezuma farewell.

drawing that his scouts had sent him showing the location of the newly arrived fleet. Hoping to tempt the newcomer over to his side, he ordered his chiefs to give Narváez gold.

For three days Montezuma kept the news about Narváez to himself. But he knew that at any moment Cortes might learn of the arrival of the ships, and he decided it would be wise to tell the Spaniard most of what he knew before he could be accused of having been personally involved in a plot with Narváez. With a display of friendly concern, Montezuma then told Cortes that the fleet had arrived, and he also suggested that now Cortes would not have to wait for new ships to be built for his departure from Mexico. Cortes agreed that this might be possible and tried to appear pleased.

However, once he was alone with his men, Cortes admitted the seriousness of the news. He was certain that the fleet could have been sent by no one but Velásquez and that his life and the lives of his companions were at stake.

Haste and boldness were called for, but first Cortes sought to assure himself that he had the support of the men who were with him. He called them together and gave them gifts of gold and other treasures, receiving in return oaths of unswerving loyalty.

In the meantime Narváez had sent a priest to parley with Sandoval at Villa Rica de Vera Cruz. The young captain met with the priest but refused to surrender the town. Nor would he listen to the proclamations that Narváez had ordered read to Sandoval and his men. Instead, Sandoval captured the men accompanying the priest and hustled them off to Tenochtitlán. Bound in net hammocks, they were relayed across the countryside on the backs of Indians. When Narváez's envoys neared Tenochtitlán they were met by deputies of Cortes who released them and led them into the city.

Gifts of native gold and European currency were used as bribes by both Cortes and Narváez. This 1543 coin bears the profile of Spain's King Charles I, who also ruled the Holy Roman Empire as Charles V.

For two days Cortes paid court to these men. He flattered them, cajoled them, and presented them with gifts. Then, satisfied that he had dazzled them, Cortes sent the envoys back to Narváez, where they could tell stories about the magnificence of the city, about how they had been treated, and about the generosity of Cortes and the faithfulness of his men.

Soon thereafter, Cortes and his captains sent messages to Narváez by Indian runners. The conquistadors explained that they were few in number and sought only the best for Spain and God. Cortes asked Narváez not to stir up trouble in Tenochtitlán and not to throw his support to Montezuma. He explained that an uprising in the already restless city would mean the destruction not only of Cortes and his men but also of Narváez and his troops. Narváez read the letter and tossed it away, even more convinced that he and his followers could easily overwhelm Cortes.

Ayllón, the representative of the Royal Audience who had sailed with Narváez, remained Cortes' champion. He pressed for an understanding between the rival camps and insisted that Cortes be assured his rights of conquest. It was, after all, Cortes who had first penetrated the rich Aztec lands. It was Cortes who had established the first Spanish settlement on the Mexican mainland in the name of the king.

Narváez not only ignored Ayllón's arguments, he ordered the emissary placed on a ship and sent at once to Spain as a prisoner. However, Ayllón managed to win over the captain of the ship, and the course was set for Santo

An elegant and courtly young man, Pedro de Alvarado was twenty-four when he sailed with Cortes in 1519. At first Montezuma was so fond of the ruddy captain that he called him "the Sun." But when Alvarado was left in charge of the emperor upon Cortes' departure, their fine relationship deteriorated. In the posthumous portrait at right, Alvarado wears the red armband of the Spanish Order of Santiago.

MUSEO NACIONAL DE HISTORIA, CHAPULTEPEC, MEXICO, D.F.

This part of the Tlaxcalan canvas shows Cortes and a Spanish force (at the left) riding to intercept Narváez. They are being guided by faithful Indians (as the Tlaxcalans always pictured themselves) and watched by native warriors, one of whom wears a wolf's-head helmet.

Domingo. There, Ayllón hoped to have the council condemn Narváez.

Once he had rid himself of the royal representative, Narváez moved his camp to Cempoala, where Cortes had paused many months before. The Cempoalans took little time to decide that Narváez had a very impressive force, and they quickly switched loyalties despite the fact that the new arrivals were a demanding, undisciplined lot.

Following in detail what was happening along the coast, Cortes and his captains decided that they should not wait for Narváez to flush them out of Tenochtitlán or allow him to disrupt the Indian alliance. Instead, they would take him by surprise and, hopefully, defeat him.

Pedro de Alvarado, the giant captain who had sailed with Grijalva and marched across Mexico with Cortes, was placed in command at Tenochtitlán. A redheaded, quick-tempered man, Alvarado was to prove one of Cortes' great mistakes. Cortes left Alvarado the major part of his army to hold, or if necessary defend, the Spanish position in the Aztec capital.

Warning his captain that Montezuma was to be held at all costs as their only protection against three thousand angry Aztecs, Cortes marched out of the city. Now he had to face an army of his own countrymen who had been sent to capture him and break his hold on Mexico.

While he was hurrying toward the coast, Cortes was rejoined by Velásquez de Leon, a relative of the governor's, who had sailed with Cortes' original expedition and was returning from a colonization mission to eastern Mexico. Though he had opposed the captain general at first, he later became a loyal supporter. With him were 120 men. Cortes had also written to Sandoval, asking the young captain to join forces with him as soon as possible.

A few days later, Sandoval rode into Cortes' camp, bringing with him those soldiers from Villa Rica de Vera Cruz who could fight, as well as five men who had deserted Narváez. Sandoval reported that he had sent two Spanish spies disguised as Indians into the Narváez camp. The men had scouted the camp thoroughly and then had ridden out on two of Narváez's horses.

Cortes and those with him laughed. There was little enough they could find funny at this moment in a situation that every day was becoming more desperate. Along with boldness and armed force, Cortes realized he would have to use every trick at his command—including bluffing. With his captains he drafted another letter. In outraged tones it denounced Narváez and his force as rebels against the crown. Cortes also informed the newcomers that they should present themselves at his camp and acknowledge his position as the representative of the king.

Narváez and his officers considered the letter to be "the ravings of mad men." It convinced Narváez that he could outwit Cortes. He suggested that Cortes parley with him at an Indian farm that stood between the two camps. The priest who had delivered Cortes' message appeared to go along with Narváez's suggestion, even though he suspected Narváez planned to break the truce and capture the captain general and his officers. Cortes knew of the plot as soon as the priest returned.

Meanwhile Cortes was preparing for the battle that appeared inevitable. He sent for some well-made Indian lances that were especially long, and he trained his men to use them. He took muster of his encampment to learn just how many men with him were able to fight. There were only 266—including the drummer and the piper. There were only five horsemen and two cannon. They faced a force of over 800 men.

As soon as the men were rested, Cortes decided there was no longer any reason to wait. They began the march on Narváez. The drummer rolled the beat, and the small column marched double-time down the road toward Cempoala. They spent the first night sleeping on the bank of a small stream. Morning found them on the road again. At midday they stopped to rest at the Antigua River.

The next day, as the march continued, the column met the scouts Cortes had sent ahead to bribe and disrupt the Narváez camp. They had had enough success to encourage the small army and to add a few more fighting men to their ranks, but the odds against them were still overwhelming— more than three to one.

The column set out on the road once more, stopping to rest for the night beside a stream about three miles from Cempoala. The men thought of the battle they would have to fight the next day—a battle different from any other they had fought since their arrival in Mexico. This time it would be Spaniard against Spaniard, Christian against Christian, steel against steel. Each side would have horses, and each side would know the ability of the other. There was very little sleeping that night as the men confessed and prepared themselves for death in a situation that seemed to offer hope of little else.

Narváez gathered little by little that Cortes had sent presents and bribes to disrupt his camp. Perturbed by the possibility of unrest or desertion, the stocky commander decided to prepare for an advance. He alerted his men, ordered the horses readied for battle, and set out extra guards. The cacique who reigned at Cempoala had kept his own scouts on the road, and they brought back the news that Cortes was on the way. The cacique, who had willingly let his town be taken over by Narváez, now panicked. He warned Narváez that Cortes was coming and would fall upon the town when he least suspected it. The Spanish general listened to the warning and laughed at the cacique's fears. Confident of an easy victory, he marched his large force out of Cempoala onto a nearby plain where the horses could easily maneuver and the heavy cannon could be brought to bear. Then he and his men settled back to wait for Cortes.

Shortly after Narváez took the field it began to rain. The day was long and wet, and the soldiers, fresh from easy lives in Cuba, were not used to such discomfort. Late in the day they began to grumble. There was no need for so many of them to get soaked while awaiting a column so small it could be crushed like a gnat. Let the horsemen cover the roads and patrol the courtyard; let the eighteen cannoneers set up their heavy artillery before the houses at Cempoala; and let the rest of them get out of the storm. Narváez finally

The priests who accompanied Cortes and other conquistadors were occasionally used for diplomatic and administrative purposes. But their main function was to convert the Indians. The row of priestly heads opposite and the baptism scene above are from an Aztec manuscript.

agreed, and the long column marched back to Cempoala. But before disbanding his men, Narváez briefed them on the signals that were to be used in case of a surprise attack. During the battle they were to yell *"Santa Maria, Santa Maria"* so that they could tell their friends from the rebel attackers under Cortes. Narváez also offered a reward of two thousand pesos to the man who killed Cortes.

Yet even at that moment Cortes had broken camp and was nearing Cempoala. A short distance from the town, he called his men together and spoke to them.

Some of you talked of returning to Cuba, but let bygones be bygones, our staying was a good thing and has furthered His Majesty's interests. . . . Let us remember, too, what we have gone through, battles and the fear of death, and what hardships . . . Think of the fifty that have died and of all those that have been wounded. . . .

And now Narváez calls us traitors . . . arrests one of the King's high officers, and has outlawed us . . . One of the two of us must quit. But . . . the past proves your courage, and now we must fight for all our property, for life, for our honor and the King's.

A half century later Bernal Díaz del Castillo could only say of that speech, "I am assuredly unable to write the like, so delightful it was and so full of promises. . . ." When Cortes finished speaking, his companions assured him that they would conquer or die, and in their fervor they warned the captain general that if he attempted to come to terms with Narváez, they would consider it betrayal and kill him.

Then Cortes explained his plan. They would move in silence, capture the artillery, prevent the cavalry from maneuvering, and then take Narváez himself. Sixty men were ordered to take the artillery and then rush the quarters of Narváez, which were reported to be in the main temple. Sandoval and sixty men were to strike directly at Narváez. To assure that there would be no diversion from this plan, Cortes offered three thousand pesos to the man who first laid hands on the enemy captain, two thousand to the second, and one thousand to the third. Two other captains were given commands of sixty men each with orders to strike at Narváez's deputies. Cortes himself kept twenty men at his side prepared for any emergency. When everything was ready Cortes told his men that their signal for recognition was *"Espiritu Santo, Espiritu Santo"* ("Holy Spirit, Holy Spirit"). Then they marched out into the darkness, their drums and trumpets muffled.

The rain continued to fall as Cortes advanced. The scouts

Though an able and dutiful soldier, Narváez was no match for Cortes in leadership, ability, or tactics. His blinded eye bandaged, Narváez (above) appears resigned as Cortes' men chain him, and batter at his stronghold with cannon.

91

ranged stealthily ahead and quickly reached the river where Narváez had set two sentries. One of the sentries was caught before he could cry out, but the other ran into the darkness shouting, "Cortes is coming. To arms! To arms."

In Cempoala, Narváez and his men tumbled out of their cots and prepared to fight, but they were too late. Before most of them could mount their horses, Cortes' men were upon them. Only four of the heavy guns were fired before the cannoneers were overwhelmed. Forced back into their quarters by the ferocity of the assault, Narváez and his men loosed a barrage of arrows and gunshot over the camp. Then Sandoval and his sixty men charged the steps of the temple that Narváez had fortified. The defense was strong, and Narváez moved down the steps to cross swords with his attackers. Then the soldiers who had captured the cannon joined forces with Sandoval, and the cries of "*Santa Maria*" and "*Espiritu Santo*" rang through the rainy night.

Suddenly Narváez fell back into the temple shrieking "*Santa Maria*, they have killed me. They have destroyed my eye!" The long pikes that Cortes had brought to the battle had taken their toll.

The men with Cortes shouted their victory, but those

Minute details in the scene of Cortes' capture of Narváez from the Tlaxcalan canvas give it the quality of an eyewitness report: a Cempoalan Indian offers flowers to the Spaniard who is putting Narváez in chains; the Tlaxcalan officer, identified as Zihuatiotzin, orders his men to haul in the Spaniards' packs; at top a horseman arrives with a message on a stick saying that Mexico City is under attack.

who stood behind Narváez were not yet ready to surrender. Sword against sword and pike against pike, the battle continued until one of the men with Cortes set fire to Narváez's headquarters, forcing his soldiers out of the temple. In a few minutes the battle was over. Narváez was taken prisoner, and his men were disarmed.

Yet among Cortes' men there was no rejoicing. Four of their comrades had been killed, and many were wounded. Weary and sweaty under their armor, they stood guard over their prisoners and waited for their dauntless captain general to decide how to proceed.

In addition to his blinded eye, Narváez suffered from multiple body wounds. Sandoval allowed his camp surgeon to look after him. When the two captain generals met, Narváez commented that Cortes must feel proud of his victory over a vastly superior armed force. But Cortes only shook his head. He was pleased that he had won, but he felt that capturing Narváez was the least glorious thing he had done in Mexico.

That same day two thousand Indian warriors arrived to help Cortes, but they saw that their assistance was no longer needed. Cortes gave them thanks and gifts and sent them back to their towns.

To assure himself that word of his victory would not reach Cuba, Cortes ordered the ships of the Narváez fleet beached and stripped. The captains and pilots were to be brought to Villa Rica de Vera Cruz. When this was done, he commanded that all of the men who had come with Narváez be set free except the general himself and one of his officers. There was some grumbling at Cortes' leniency, and one of his captains said openly that he resented the presents that had been distributed among the newcomers. As always, Cortes was able to quiet his own men with praise and kind words. To the newcomers he promised a share in the conquest, and as they had very little choice in the matter, they agreed to follow him.

It was at this moment of victory, when Cortes must have begun again to dream of a New World empire secure under the cross and the banner of Spain, that he received word that everything had suddenly gone against him in Tenochtitlán. The entire city was in revolt against the Spaniards, who were surrounded and besieged. Their quarters had been burned down, and seven men had been killed and many others wounded. Alvarado needed help, and he needed it at once. Without delay, Cortes sent Narváez to Villa Rica de Vera Cruz under guard.

Lienzo de Tlaxcalla, CHAVERO, 1892

A nineteenth-century copyist made this recapitulation of the authentic scene opposite—bouquet and all.

VI THE SAD NIGHT

BIBLIOTECA NACIONAL, MADRID

Alvarado and his men were forced to take refuge in their quarters after they made an attack on the Aztecs. In this contemporary drawing they defend themselves with harquebuses and crossbows against besieging Indians who include two members of the elite warrior class—an eagle knight (center) and a jaguar knight (second from right)—distinguished by their colorful animal costumes.

94

The news of Cortes' victory in the east quickly reached the Aztec capital, and a few days later the loyal Tlaxcalans told Cortes that the attacks on Alvarado's men in Tenochtitlán had stopped. The situation was calm for the moment, though the Spanish garrison was dejected and hungry.

Cortes listened to the reports of the Tlaxcalans and ordered a muster so that he could determine how many men he had with him for the march back into the angry city. The force now under his command was the largest he had yet assembled. There were over a thousand Spanish soldiers and more than eighty horses. In addition, two thousand Tlaxcalan warriors agreed to accompany Cortes.

When the long column arrived at Texcoco, the highly civilized Aztec city on the east side of Lake Texcoco, they found silence. There were no caciques to meet them, and most of the townspeople had hidden themselves away. Without pausing or waiting for an escort, Cortes marched once more along the causeway into the great capital itself. No one whom the Spaniards knew came out to welcome them. There was no one on the streets. As far as they could tell, the houses were empty. Soldier looked at soldier and each held his weapons a little tighter. Those who had been under the command of Narváez looked about in wonder, for the strange city on the lake was fully as marvelous as they had heard.

Cortes (mounted, at left) leads his forces into Tenochtitlán to raise the siege of Alvarado's garrison.

Not until they reached the walls of the compound they had occupied before did the Spaniards see any signs of life. As they entered the courtyard they saw Alvarado's guards posted on the flat roofs of the buildings within the compound. Montezuma came forward to greet Cortes, but the captain general received him coldly. Cortes knew that Montezuma had encouraged Narváez's treachery, and that the Aztec ruler could have ordered food sent to Alvarado and his beleaguered men at the time of the uprising. Montezuma understood Cortes' anger, and he returned to his quarters with the knowledge that the game they had been playing was over. Montezuma was not Cortes' honored guest—he was a prisoner.

After he had arranged for the lodging and feeding of his large force, Cortes demanded that Alvarado explain the cause of the uprising and the death of seven men. Alvarado said that during an Aztec festival he had been informed that the Indians planned to attack him as soon as the ceremonies were ended. Deciding to act first, he struck quickly and forcefully. When the battle ended, there were nearly six hundred dead Aztec leaders and priests.

It has never been clear whether Alvarado's version of the slaughter was correct or whether he had been trying some dubious scheme of conquest on his own. Cortes himself glossed over this incident in his letter to the king, but it is certain that he was not pleased with Alvarado. He told the captain as much, and then put the causes of the uprising aside to deal with the results.

The Aztecs of Tenochtitlán seemed less willing than ever to settle down to a tranquil acceptance of Spanish rule. As Cortes wrote of the day that followed his return to Tenochtitlán:

The next day after mass I sent a messenger to Villa Rica de Vera

Cruz to give them the good news that the Christians were alive and that I was safe in the city. Within half an hour the messenger returned with his head all bruised and broken, calling out that the Indians in the city were in battle array and had raised all the bridges. Immediately such a great multitude fell upon us from all sides that neither the roofs nor the houses could be seen in the crowd, which came on with the most frightful yells. With their slings they threw so many stones into the fortress that it seemed as if they rained from the heavens. The arrows and missiles were so thick, and so filled the buildings and courts, that we could hardly move about. I sallied forth against them on two or three sides, and they fought us most valiantly. In one place where a captain had gone out with two hundred men, they wounded him and many others and killed four before he could withdraw. On the other side where I was engaged, they wounded me and many other Spaniards.

We killed few of them, for they retreated to the other side of the bridges and did us great injury with stones from the roofs and terraces. We captured some terraces and set them on fire; but they were so many and so strong, and so filled with people well supported with stones and other weapons, that we were not strong enough to take them all nor to defend ourselves when it pleased them to attack. They assailed the fort so violently and set fire to it in so many places that on one side a great part was destroyed before we stopped it by breaking the walls and pulling down a part, which put out the fire. Had it not been for the strong guard of gunners and archers, with some field pieces that I placed there, they would have scaled that part without our being able to resist them. We fought this way all that day until night was well advanced, and even throughout the night they kept up their cries and yells.

The long night that followed the first day of battle was the first of many such nights. Breaches in the walls had to be repaired and strengthened, guards and sentries set, and the wounded patched up well enough to fight the next day. All through the sleepless night the conquistadors could hear the Indians yelling outside the walls of their small compound.

When dawn broke, an even fiercer battle began. Cortes and his captains left the safety of the walled fortress to meet the Indians in the open streets. The Spaniards dragged some of their cannon with them, and pointing the artillery down the long avenues that led to the causeways, they tried to clear a path with heavy shot and ball, but in this and other conventional battle tactics they failed. There were so many Aztec warriors that the gaps left by their fallen companions were quickly filled as the natives continued the onslaught against the invaders.

Again the Spaniards attacked, killing thirty or forty
warriors, and again they had to fall back before the press
of the Aztec troops. Several times the Indians retreated,
but Cortes held his men in check, knowing that the Aztecs
were trying to lure them away from the protection of their
fortress. In desperation he tried a new tactic; he ordered
his men to burn the houses that lined the main avenue.
However, between each large house there was a canal or an
inlet from the lake, and the fire would not spread from
house to house. The small bridges across the canals had
already been withdrawn, and in order to move forward the
Spaniards had to wade through deep water while the Aztecs hurled stones down upon them from the roof tops.
Unable to gain any advantage, Cortes withdrew once more
to the compound. A dozen conquistadors were dead, and
all of the others were wounded. Those who had fought in
Europe or against the Turks said they had never seen such
a battle, nor had they ever met men with the courage of
the Aztec warriors.

Popular resentment against the presence of the Span-

*Montezuma (on balcony opposite) was stoned by his angry subjects when he
asked them to make peace with the Spaniards. The Indians were seeking revenge for the massacre at the feast of Toxcatl (above) five weeks earlier.*

98

ycq̃tla tí tetȝavitl
yn mal ques.

Fierce street fighting broke out after Cortes re-entered Tenochtitlán. Above, during the struggle, Spanish cavalry and foot soldiers, backed by Indian allies, storm up the steps to the roof of the temple.

iards in Tenochtitlán was now beyond the control of any government. Originally Cortes had thought that the conquistadors' only protection against the Aztecs was the authority of Montezuma. Cortes now realized that he had overestimated Montezuma's imperial authority and had underestimated the Aztecs' driving will to rid themselves of the humiliation of foreign rule.

For the next two days, the Spaniards remained in their quarters. The unfortunate Tlaxcalans, who slept in the open courtyard, were under a constant barrage of stones and arrows. Many of these missiles were shot from the high temple that overlooked the Spanish compound— the same temple where only a few months before Cortes had erected a Christian altar. During these two days,

100

Cortes and his men built a small movable tower that could be pushed into battle to protect soldiers using firearms. They were determined to capture the high temple where the Aztecs sacrificed to their god of war—Huitzilopochtli.

At dawn the besieged conquistadors moved out of their quarters, pushing the tower before them. But the way was soon blocked by thousands of Aztec warriors and by impenetrable barricades. Again the Spaniards were forced to fight without protection in the open streets. They battled from house to house, attacking and falling back, and attacking once more until they reached the base of the high temple. Over four thousand Aztecs were massed at the base of the pyramid, and at least five hundred more were guarding the summit.

Step by step Cortes and a few of his companions fought their way to the top while the rest of the soldiers fought at the base. The lower levels of the pyramid were covered with slick flagstones, and the horses, having difficulty keeping their footing, fell heavily. But Cortes pushed on, finally fighting his way to the flat area at the top of the temple.

Here a vicious struggle took place. Each of the enemy forces strove to drive the other over the precipitous sides of the high temple. The losers fell, crushed below. Cortes himself was forced to the very edge, but he fought free and continued to lead his men. Soon the Spaniards were alone at the very top. The enemy dead lay about them or had been hurled from the heights. Cortes ordered his men to burn the place where the pagan idols were housed, and they toppled the large statue of the god of war down the hundreds of steps and watched it crash below.

Horrified by the destruction of their gods, the Aztecs stood stunned at the base of the pyramid. Cortes took advantage of this moment to withdraw from a position in which he and his men might have been trapped. Finally, and with great relief, they reached the safety of their quarters. Sixteen had been killed or captured for sacrifice, and everyone else had been wounded.

Cortes wrote that he "returned to the fort with infinite sorrow." Bernal Díaz, remembering that battle in later years, wrote, "Oh! what a fight and what a fierce battle it was that took place; it was a memorable thing to see us all streaming with blood and covered with wounds and others slain."

That night passed as had the others; the Indians outside the walls screaming for revenge, the living burying their dead companions, all bandaging their wounds. The

guards were alert, and the horses were bitted and waiting.

Though ready to continue the battle, Cortes had concluded that there was no way he could fight his way to victory in the city. Each Aztec warrior killed was replaced by another, each neighborhood conquered was lost the following night. And in his own camp there was unrest. Those who had come to Mexico with Narváez felt Cortes had betrayed them with his promises of easy wealth. Those who had come to the city with Cortes the first time knew that the odds against them were insurmountable. They had to leave immediately if they could.

When he saw his men were crumbling under the strain of battle, Cortes turned to Montezuma for help. He asked the emperor to speak to his people. Reluctantly, Montezuma mounted the flat roof of the tallest building of the compound. His Spanish guards were at his side as he addressed the thousands of warriors who gathered in the streets to hear him. Most of his captains and caciques were there. The war captains stood silent with their men as the

The true cause of Montezuma's death may never be known. The Indians accused the Spaniards of murdering him because his usefulness was ended; the Spaniards claimed he was killed by the stoning he received from his own people. Later they threw the dead emperor and one of his chiefs into a canal (opposite) and prepared to leave the city. The panel at right, painted by a seventeenth-century Spanish artist, depicts the conquistadors' retreat.

emperor asked them to allow the Spaniards to leave. But when he had finished, a shout went up from the caciques telling Montezuma that they had chosen a new emperor and that they would not stop fighting until all of the invaders were dead. Then a shower of arrows and stones fell over the roof. One stone struck Montezuma on the head.

The Spaniards led him below and tried to care for him, but Montezuma, despairing and dishonored, would not be helped. The enemies of Cortes later claimed that he killed the emperor because Montezuma was no longer of any use as a prisoner. No one really knows what happened. As Bernal Díaz reported the incident: "The men with Montezuma pleaded with him to have his wounds tended and to eat, and though they spoke kindly to him, he refused. Then to our surprise, those who had been with him reported that he was dead. Cortes, his captains, and his soldiers wept for him." Cortes' comment in his dispatch to the king was even more brief: "One of his own subjects hit him on the head with such force that within three days he died. I had his body taken out by two of the Indian prisoners, but I do not know what his people did with him." The great Montezuma, who in a reign of seventeen years had brought one of the richest civilizations of the world to its height, was dead.

Although retreat was the only choice the conquistadors now had, they were appalled by the very thought of it. Cortes began his move to leave the capital by releasing a number of prisoners with the message that all he wanted was a safe passage out of the city. For this concession, he was prepared to abandon all of the treasure he had amassed in Mexico. The Aztec chieftains scornfully refused to accept this offer.

At the same time, he ordered his men to build a strong portable bridge to replace the ones over the causeways that the Indians had demolished. During the retreat he planned to cross over the open sections of the causeway by dragging the bridge from gap to gap.

Planning with great care, he and his men decided to take a roundabout route out of the city, which would enable them to cross the shortest causeway and which would, they hoped, have fewer guards than the main routes. There was much discussion as to whether they should try to withdraw at night, when the enemy might be less likely to attack, or during the day, when they themselves could see what they were doing. A soldier who knew astrology checked the stars and recommended that they move out at night.

Cortes organized his withdrawal with characteristic boldness and care: forty men were to carry the bridge; fifty soldiers were to drag the cannon; Sandoval was to lead the way with two hundred of the most able-bodied men; Cortes and the other captains were to ride in the middle of the column, shifting their support to points where it might be needed the most; and Alvarado was to bring up the rear guard. Doña Marina and Montezuma's children were to remain in the middle of the column, where it was believed they would be safest.

Then the bags of gold and valuables were brought from the treasury and placed in the middle of the floor. The royal representatives were told to take the king's share, or as much of it as they could, and prepare to move it out on seven wounded horses. An enormous treasure in gold, silver, and ornaments remained. With cynical generosity, Cortes told his men to pick up whatever they wanted rather than leave it for the Indians. But he warned them that those who traveled lightest would have the best chance for survival. The older soldiers who had come into Mexico with him selected a few valuable jewels and left the rest to the newcomers, who were more greedy and inexperienced. The Narváez men loaded themselves down with so many gold and silver ingots and so much other plunder that they could barely walk.

Outside it was dark. Rain had begun to fall, and a mist had risen from the lake and spread over the city. The gates of the compound were flung open, and the column began to march out into the street. The only noises were the muffled steps of men and horses on stone. The Aztecs appeared to be asleep. Slowly the column made its way to the first gap in the great causeway. The bridge was set into place and the vanguard crossed over to the other side. Then suddenly out of the darkness Aztec sentries began to shout, alerting their companions. Shell trumpets were sounded, and the drums on top of the temple began to rumble. From that moment on everything was confusion.

Aztec canoes loaded with warriors crowded into the lake on both sides of the causeway. They trapped the Spaniards between them and showered arrows into the retreating column. Horses slipped on the wet stones and fell into the lake. The Indians swarmed over the rear of the retreating column, killing everyone they could reach. Alvarado, leading the rear guard, tried to hold them back until the bridge could be lifted and then moved ahead to fill the next gap in the causeway, but none of his efforts succeeded. The

TEXT CONTINUED ON PAGE 108

Four illustrations from Sahagún's history (opposite) narrate Cortes' flight from Tenochtitlán. At top the Spaniards, with a rear guard of Tlaxcalan allies, leave their quarters. Next, a woman drawing water from a canal observes their escape and raises the alarm, which is repeated by a man on the temple steps. In the third drawing, Aztec warriors in canoes attack conquistadors as they cross a causeway. Last, the bodies of Spanish and Indian dead fill a gap in the causeway.

Hostile Indians made frequent attacks on the Spaniards as they retreated to friendly Tlaxcalan territory. Led by an officer (right of center) bearing a

shield emblazoned with the red cross of the Order of Santiago de Compostella, possibly Cortes himself, the weary invaders fight their way out of an ambush.

TEXT CONTINUED FROM PAGE 105

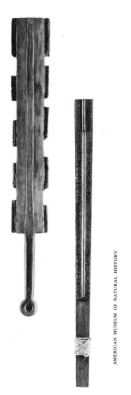

The favorite weapons of the Aztecs were the macuahuitl (above at left), a yard-long club edged with flint or obsidian, and the atlatl (at right), a spear thrower about two feet long.

AMERICAN MUSEUM OF NATURAL HISTORY

horsemen and troops who had marched over the bridge had set it firmly in place, and no amount of effort could remove it. Sandoval, in the vanguard, faced other hordes of Indians rushing toward them from the other end of the causeway, and he had trouble moving forward. Then bodies of men and horses began to fill up the second gap in the causeway, forming a bridge. Cortes and those with him pressed forward. But others, weighted down by the gold they had so greedily taken, fell into the lake, where they drowned or were taken prisoner by the attacking Aztecs. No one could hear the shouted orders of Cortes over the din of the battle, and every man struck out for himself.

Unable to hold the rear any longer, Alvarado raced to the gap in the causeway and used his lance to vault to the section beyond. Afterwards there were those who said he could not have done this, but the place where he vaulted became known as Alvarado's Leap. The men with him who could not follow were either struck down where they fought or were taken prisoner.

After what may have been hours, Cortes reached the relative safety of the far end of the causeway. However, the fighting continued to rage behind him, and he turned back to rescue any of his men who might still be alive. As he rode into the fury once more, he met Alvarado, badly wounded but still holding his lance. The huge soldier was accompanied by four Spaniards and eight Tlaxcalans—all that remained of the rear guard. Cortes rallied the remnants of his army and continued the desperate fight along the causeway.

Nearing Tacuba, the Aztec village located at the end of the causeway, the captain general found the natives there preparing to block his retreat. But he hurled his badly mauled troops at them, and they made their way to a hill outside the village and rested briefly. Cortes looked over his men and assessed his losses. All of his prisoners were dead, including the sons and daughters of Montezuma. Most of those who had arrived from Cuba with Narváez were either dead or prisoners of the Aztecs. Only twenty-three horses had been rescued. All of his men were wounded. The cannon, powder, and firearms were all gone. No one knows how many Tlaxcalans died crossing the lake. But the veteran conquistadors had brought Doña Marina through alive.

It had been a terrible night, probably the worst Cortes and those with him were ever to spend. Most of the treasure was gone. About four hundred and fifty Spaniards had died and perhaps as many as four thousand Indians. As significant as anything else, the full Spanish force had been beaten. Badly outnumbered by the Aztec warriors, they had been driven out of Tenochtitlán. Cortes was to remember the night with "infinite sorrow." History was to call it the *noche triste*—the woeful night.

·Yet the ordeal of Cortes was not over. He and his companions were still deep in Aztec territory and surrounded by enemies.

At midnight, leaving his campfires burning, Cortes moved his column away from Tacuba. He had hoped to leave in secret, but Aztec sentries discovered the Spaniards' departure. Throughout the rest of the night and the next day, Cortes and his men had to fight their way across the countryside, taking a circuitous route around the lakes that they hoped would keep them clear of the most populous Aztec centers.

For six days the Spaniards retreated, and they had to fight every step of the way. More Spaniards died, some of hunger, some in battle. As Cortes recalled it later: "My men were exhausted with hunger and thirst, and the horses were well tired out. We continued our march and suffered great trouble and fatigue, for we lost our way many times." On the morning of the seventh day they reached the mountain rampart that overlooks the plain of Otumba. Though their course around the lakes was much farther, they had only traveled about twenty-three miles from the city toward the sea.

As they descended into the valley of Otumba, the conquistadors thought they saw something strange in the distance. And as they approached the valley they realized that their path was blocked by the largest Aztec force that had yet been assembled against them. As far as a man could see, Aztec warriors filled the valley. Plumed, helmeted, and armed, they waited for Cortes and the remnants of his army.

There was no turning back toward the enemy capital because that way lay destruction. Cortes looked about at his own soldiers: many a man had only a sword to protect him, most were too weary to stand, and there were too few horses left to make any difference in battle. But, in spite of the overwhelming odds, the determined captain general knew there was only one thing left to do—attack! He must attempt to cut a swath through the thousands of Indians blocking his escape.

Cortes spoke to his small band of conquistadors and

This Indian warrior is armed with a long-handled club called a cuau-hololli, which was not a common weapon among Aztecs but was used by the tribes they had conquered.

spurred them to battle once again. They prayed and then moved forward. For a time it looked as if they would be overwhelmed by the mass of enemy troops. The crush was so great that it was no longer an army facing a few soldiers, but man facing man, killing and moving on to another man. Yet despite the many Aztecs they killed, the Spaniards could only inch forward because they were actually cutting their way deeper into the sea of enemy warriors. They fought for hours. The sun rose high and scorched the plain of Otumba. Leaving in its wake the dead and dying bodies, the battle moved on. By midday every Spaniard had a fresh wound, but none who could still wield a sword gave up the fight through fear or resignation. They knew that their survival meant bettering the enemy in each moment-by-moment encounter. Thrusting and stumbling, and then thrusting again, the end was nearly at hand for the conquistadors who had so boldly dared to invade an empire.

Then, in the distance, Cortes saw an Aztec chief wear-

Cortes' firm leadership, plus his usual luck and the skill and discipline of his men, made it possible for him to defeat a vast Aztec army in the valley of Otumba. This engraving shows the Spaniards (far right) filing over the crest of a sierra to face the enemy divisions (at far left) gathered on the plain.

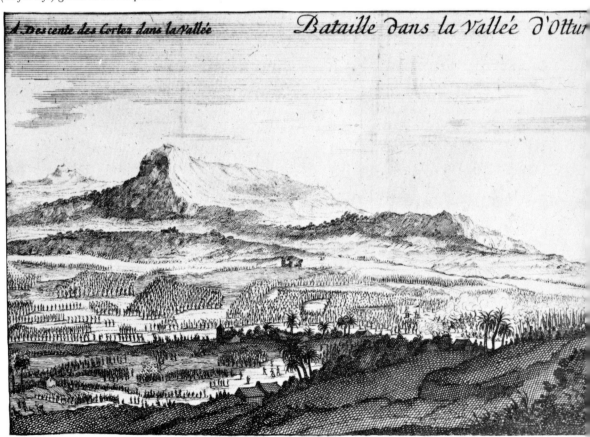

A Descente des Cortez dans la Vallée

Bataille dans la Vallée d'Ottur

110

ing a brightly colored cloak and a high, plumed headdress. Gathering his captains—Sandoval, Alvarado, Olid, and Avila—Cortes hurled himself toward the leader of the Indian armies. Stunned by the sudden fury of the assault, the Aztecs fell away for a moment, and in that instant Cortes and his captains killed the chief. The guards who had been set to protect their leader fled from the field. Their panic spread, and in a few minutes Cortes and his men were forgotten as the Aztecs thought only of escape— trampling one another in their haste. Weary as the Spaniards were, they followed, seeking revenge for the humiliation of their long retreat. When night fell, the field belonged to Cortes and the few fighting men who survived with him.

The Battle of Otumba was fought on July 7, 1520. The victorious Spaniards would never forget it; nor would the Aztecs forget the humiliation of their loss. In the days that followed, the Aztecs watched Cortes withdraw to Tlaxcala. They knew he was not defeated.

B. General des Mexiquains.

THE ROUTE TO VICTORY

Cortes had allies in Tlaxcala who were prepared to stand by him in need. For twenty-two days the captain general and his men rested and recovered from their wounds. During this period, Montezuma's successor died of small-pox, and Cuauhtémoc, a young man of about twenty-five and Montezuma's nephew, ascended the Aztec throne. The young ruler sent messengers with rich offers to the caciques of Tlaxcala. He was prepared to give them whatever they might want if they would turn against the Spaniards. He promised. He threatened. But the Tlaxcalans remained loyal in spite of the fact that Cortes had salvaged almost none of the Aztec treasure and had little to offer his allies.

When Cortes thought his men sufficiently rested, he decided to give additional battle experience to those soldiers who had joined him from Narváez's army. He was determined to raise the prestige of the Spanish troops to the heights it had held before the flight from Mexico. He felt that the best way to do this would be to attack and subdue the tribes that bordered Tlaxcala. The most obvious target for this campaign were the Tepeacans, who shortly before the *noche triste* had attacked and killed a dozen Spanish soldiers.

However, the soldiers who had come with Narváez objected to taking part in another campaign. They had had enough of fighting and were ready to return to Cuba. Many had families there, as well as farms or businesses. They had left home for what had appeared to be an easy adventure and a quick route to riches. Instead, they had faced the fury of the Aztecs and had lost many of their companions in the sad retreat from the fabulous city of Mexico.

The modern Mexican artist David Siqueiros portrayed Cuauhtémoc, Montezuma's nephew, wearing Spanish armor with an Aztec crown and club (left). A seventeenth-century European engraver pictured him as a raw youth (above).

When they realized that Cortes was not listening to their pleas, they drew up a formal requisition before a king's notary.

In this document they demanded that Cortes leave Tlaxcala at once, return to Villa Rica de Vera Cruz on the coast, and abandon all plans for war. Their reasons seemed logical: the horses were dead, the guns and crossbows had been lost in the retreat. All of the men were wounded, and only four hundred and forty had survived the Narváez expedition. The Mexicans held all of the fortresses, the highlands, and the passes. If Cortes delayed, the ships which lay on the coast would be worm-eaten and useless. They wanted to return, and they wanted to return at once.

Cortes read their document. He asked them if they thought it would be in the service of God and the king to desert their captain in time of war. At length Narváez's men realized that Cortes would never weaken. He still held the loyalty of those who had first come with him as well as the Tlaxcalans. The petitioners could only back down and agree to remain in New Spain on the condition that Cortes would allow them to return to Cuba when the opportunity arose.

Once this was settled, the conquistadors marched on the Tepeacans to the southeast of Tlaxcala. After a swift but brutal battle, the Spaniards overwhelmed and slew the Indian warriors. They made captives of the women and children, then branded them and distributed them among the troops. As always there was grumbling among the men that they had not received a fair share of the spoils, but Cortes managed to quiet the hot Spanish tempers.

In the same month he marched on Quechola, defeated the Indian warriors there, and again distributed the women and children as slaves.

In Tenochtitlán, Cuauhtémoc learned of the Spanish exploits with growing concern. Sending large armies to the frontier, he planned to prevent any further incursion of Spanish forces into Oaxaca or the neighboring provinces.

Cortes was kept informed of the arrival of Aztec troops and was planning his next move when he received letters from Villa Rica de Vera Cruz informing him that a ship had put into the port. She was commanded by Pedro Barba, an old and good friend of Cortes'. Although Barba's ship was tiny, he had brought with him thirteen men and two horses. In addition, he brought with him a number of letters from Velásquez to Narváez, whom all in Cuba believed to be in command on the continent. Rushed inland by Cortes' men at Villa Rica de Vera Cruz, Barba turned the dispatches over to the captain general. Velásquez's orders to Narváez were quite clear: if Narváez had not yet killed Cortes, he was to send him as a prisoner to Cuba where he would be placed aboard a vessel bound for Spain.

Thankful for the news, as well as the horses and men, Cortes named Barba a captain in his army and made his companions soldiers of New Spain. About a week later a second vessel put in at Villa Rica de Vera Cruz, and those aboard also joined Cortes. In addition to the captain there were eight soldiers, six crossbows, and a large quantity of bowstring.

While Cortes was absorbing the newly arrived soldiers, the Aztec legions of Cuauhtémoc were harassing his allies.

This section of a mural by Diego Rivera shows the gradual Spanish subjugation of the Indians. In the center natives are branded; at top they erect Spanish palaces as slave laborers; and at right a bishop is burning Aztec scrolls as Cortes stands above the flames.

PALACIO NACIONAL, MEXICO, D.F.

115

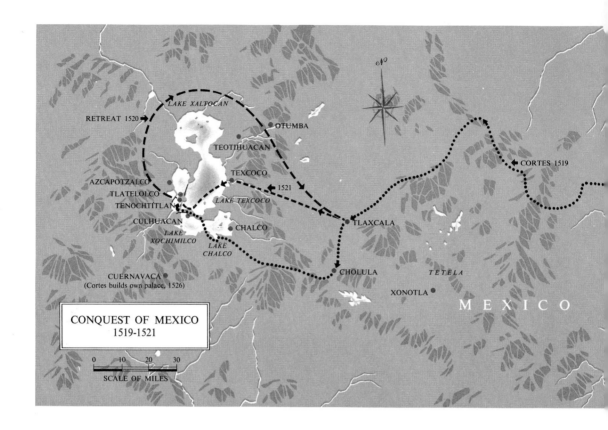

The labels on the map read:

LAKE XALTOCAN

RETREAT 1520 →

OTUMBA

TEOTIHUACAN

CORTES 1519 ←

AZCAPOTZALCO

TEXCOCO

TLATELOLCO

1521

TENOCHTITLAN

LAKE TEXCOCO

CULHUACAN

CHALCO

TLAXCALA

LAKE XOCHIMILCO

LAKE CHALCO

CUERNAVACA
(Cortes builds own palace, 1526)

CHOLULA

TETELA

XONOTLA

M E X I C O

CONQUEST OF MEXICO
1519-1521

0   10   20   30

SCALE OF MILES

The captain general sent Cristóbal de Olid on an expedition to drive the Mexicans back. In two pitched battles Olid forced the Aztecs to retreat, lost four precious horses, and was himself wounded twice. However, the Spaniards began to receive unexpected reinforcements.

When rumors of the riches in Mexico reached the ears of Francisco de Garay, the ambitious governor of the island of Jamaica, he financed an expedition to the mouth of the Pánuco River on the mainland. This venture ended in disaster, but Garay was not daunted. The following year he sent out a second expedition of a hundred and fifty men.

When this small force was attacked by Indians on the Pánuco, the captain and his sixty remaining men withdrew to the safety of Villa Rica de Vera Cruz. All were hungry, yellow with disease, and had bellies so swollen they could barely walk. They were welcomed at the coastal settlement and sent overland to join Cortes. The "yellow bellies," as they came to be called, were of little use to the captain general, for he had no doctors to heal them. However, these

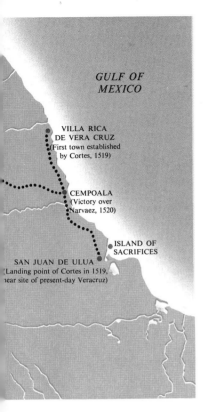

GULF OF
MEXICO

VILLA RICA
DE VERA CRUZ
(First town established
by Cortes, 1519)

CEMPOALA
(Victory over
Narvaez, 1520)

ISLAND OF
SACRIFICES

SAN JUAN DE ULUA
(Landing point of Cortes in 1519,
near site of present-day Veracruz)

Cortes' entire campaign in Mexico took no more than three years. His initial march in 1519 from Cempoala to Mexico City is shown on the map above as a dotted line. In 1520, after the battle of the noche triste, *he retreated north around the lake and east to Tlaxcala. A year later, with a renewed army, he moved to Texcoco. From there he launched his final successful assault upon the Aztecs' capital city.*

sick men had brought along badly needed equipment.

Soon afterward, the Jamaican governor sent still another expedition to relieve his Pánuco venture, and these men also found their way to Villa Rica de Vera Cruz. Their captain had paused at Pánuco just long enough to see what misfortune had overtaken his predecessors and then had sailed to join Cortes. This contingent brought fifty strong men and ten horses. A few days later yet another vessel from the small armada that Garay thought he was assembling at Pánuco found its way to Villa Rica de Vera Cruz. There were more soldiers and more horses for Cortes' army.

To season these newcomers and to impress the Indians with his growing strength, Cortes sent young Gonzalo de Sandoval on a raiding expedition. Two towns were struck, their women and children branded and distributed among the conquistadors. But the fighting was fierce. Sandoval and eight of his men were wounded, and three of the horses were killed.

In Cortes' camp Narváez's men continued to plead for permission to return to Cuba, and now that he was reestablishing control over the countryside, the captain general felt free to release them. He gave them maize, salted dogs, and a good ship. Then he sent them off to Cuba with a letter and a few ornaments and ingots of gold for his wife.

The men who remained protested at seeing their numbers cut so sharply, but Cortes explained that he wanted to be rid of the brawls and arguments that had been dividing his camp. He needed harmony and cooperation in the ranks for the final conquest of Tenochtitlán.

At the same time he released Narváez's men, Cortes sent two messengers to Spain to negotiate for him with King Charles. He sent a third messenger to Santo Domingo to tell the members of the Royal Audience what had happened to his expedition. The Royal Audience had interceded for him in his quarrel with Velásquez, and Cortes wanted to keep its continued support.

Then with all of the boldness that had marked so many of his actions, Cortes sent a representative directly to Jamaica to purchase horses. The arrival of this representative was probably the first word Garay had received that his own plans for conquest on the mainland had gone completely awry.

Cortes did not wait for word from Spain or for his additional horses to arrive. He plunged into what was to be one of the most difficult tasks he and his small band of adventurers ever undertook—the building of a fleet. None of the men who survived the *noche triste* would ever forget the effectiveness of the Aztec fleet of canoes that had cut down the helpless Spaniards as they moved across the long causeway.

Cortes moved his men back to Tlaxcala, from which they had marched out to raid and subjugate the countryside, and here he began the construction of his own fleet, using wood from the great forests around Tlaxcala. Thirteen ships were to be built in sections and hauled over the mountains to Lake Texcoco. Martín López, a soldier who had been with the expedition from the beginning, was asked to design boats that would sail swiftly over shallow waters. With the help of a few Spanish carpenters and the Tlaxcalans, he built the ships. Then he had them dismantled and each piece marked so it could be readily put in its place when the fleet was finally assembled.

Meanwhile, Cortes sent to Villa Rica de Vera Cruz for the remaining iron, anchors, bolts, rigging, sails, and canvas which had been salvaged from his scuttled fleet. With the help of a thousand Tlaxcalans all of this was hauled inland from the coast along with the cauldrons in which the ships' captains melted the pitch used to seal the joints. When the strange cargo reached Tlaxcala, Cortes sent four sailors out to make pitch in some pine woods several miles away.

When everything that he could do in Tlaxcala had been completed—his men assembled and trained, his horses rested and readied, the ship sections ready to be moved—Cortes prepared to move to Texcoco. This would be his new base of operations. From there he would lay down the siege that he hoped would end in the fall of Tenochtitlán and Mexico.

Just as he and his men were about to march inland, word came that a large ship from Spain and the Canary Islands had arrived on the coast. To the great fortune of the captain general, it was a merchant vessel whose captain had heard that he might be able to do business on the Mexican coast. He had brought with him harquebuses, bowstrings, three horses, and various other kinds of arms. Without hesitation, Cortes bought everything that was available. The crew, caught up in the excitement of the adventure that was about to take place, joined the conquistadors.

There was nothing more that Cortes needed except, perhaps, word from Spain that the king smiled on his

Crossbows were widely used by sixteenth-century forces like Cortes'. In this detail from a contemporary painting, an archer draws back his bowstring with a ratcheted winch.

118

operations. But he could not afford to wait for such news. If he was successful, he would surely have the support of the throne, and if he failed, he would not need it.

On December 28, 1520, three days after the Feast of the Nativity, Cortes left Tlaxcala at the head of an army of five hundred and fifty Spaniards, about ten thousand Indian allies, and forty horses. The next day the army was in Mexican territory. Scouts covered the countryside. A vanguard was set up to protect the long column, the cannon, and other equipment.

Finally, as Cortes remembered afterwards, "we caught sight of the lake of Mexico and its great cities standing in the water, and when we saw it, we gave thanks to God for allowing us to see it again."

As the invading army of conquistadors and their allies descended the mountain range and moved toward Lake Texcoco, they could see tall smoke signals rising from the towns below. Approaching a narrow pass through which they had to march, the Spaniards found their way blocked by a legion of Aztec warriors. The two armies met near a small wooden bridge which spanned a canyon with a waterfall below. The clash was brief and decisive. The Mexicans gave way and retreated—leaving the way clear for the continued invasion by Cortes and his men.

That night the Spaniards paused in a small village about seven miles from Texcoco. They set out their guards and waited for an attack that did not come. The next morning they started for the city—one of the largest in Mexico and the Americas. They had gone only a short distance when Cortes' scouts rode in to report that a delegation was on its way to meet with him.

Seven caciques from Texcoco came forward under banners which declared a truce. They offered their city to the invaders if Cortes would assure them that he and his allies would do them no harm.

The Spaniards argued the issue among themselves. Some of the captains were convinced this was a trick, but Cortes settled the matter by giving his promise to the caciques. Then he and his column marched into the city that controlled the southern end of the lake from whose shores they had fled months before. However, no one came out to greet the conquistadors as they entered the city. The streets were empty. Suspicious, Cortes quartered his men in the royal palace and ordered Alvarado and Olid to climb to the top of the great temple of Texcoco. From this vantage point the two captains could scan the city in the lake and

A native chronicle contains the above sketch of crossbowmen, along with this note: "They came wielding and repeatedly testing [their weapons], sighting along them."

119

the entire countryside. They saw the women and children of Texcoco fleeing from them—some going to the hills, some running down to the thickets near the lake. They saw the lake crowded with canoes, all moving away from Texcoco. The conquered city was nothing but an empty shell.

For the next twelve days Cortes, his troops, and his allies remained in Texcoco. They reconnoitered the countryside and prepared for the siege of Tenochtitlán. During these twelve days, the Tlaxcalans ate all the food they had brought with them, and when they scoured the area for more, they could not find enough to feed so many men. If Cortes was to keep his allies with him, he had to feed them, so he set forth to capture Ixtapalapa, another of the large cities in the area. Half of this town was built on dry land and half was built over the water. As the Spanish host approached, the Aztecs fought a delaying action on

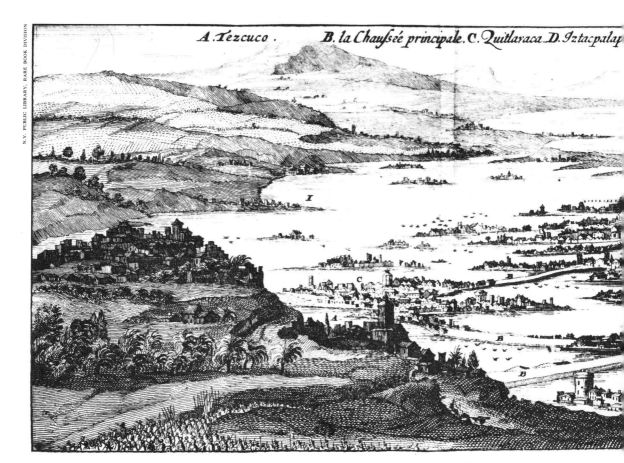

As the Spaniards prepared for their new attack on Tenochtitlán they knew that they must take the capital's beautiful but nearly impregnable loca-

dry land, falling slowly back into their city. The Spaniards and Tlaxcalans followed, entering the houses built on water and even wading through the water from house to house. Suddenly the water began to rise as a great torrent rushed through the town, sweeping almost everything before it—the Indians had smashed the dikes to trap the intruders. Struggling to free themselves, the allies scrambled for dry land. At the same time the Aztecs pounced on them from all sides. But the Spaniards fought back fiercely, and despite heavy casualties, they routed the Indians and carried the day.

For two days the Spaniards rested and planned their next move. Then on the third day emissaries appeared from two nearby towns. They had come to make peace and be forgiven for past wars. Cortes had no choice but to accept their offer of friendship. If nothing else, their act

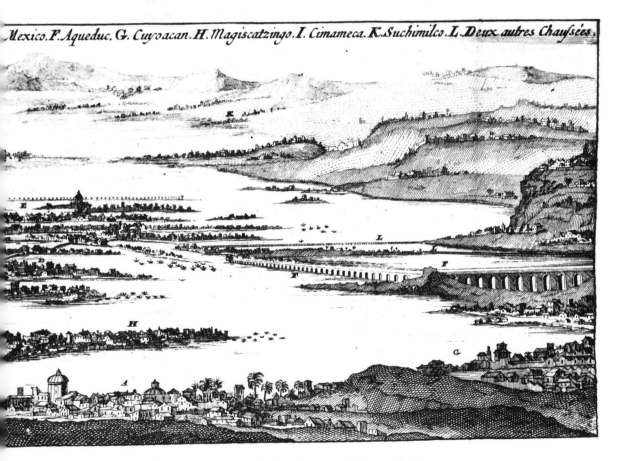

tion into account. This engraving shows the view Cortes and his men (far left) first had of the city with its main causeway (B) and aqueduct (F).

signified that Spanish arms were once more respected.

Word came that there were other towns prepared to surrender to the invaders if they could be certain of Spanish protection against the Aztecs. Cortes guaranteed this by sending out expeditions to help them cut their ties with Tenochtitlán.

Confident that he had secured his base of operations, Cortes sent Indian emissaries to Cuauhtémoc offering him peace. First he made threats. Once a war between them started, he said, it would lead to total destruction—the city would be wiped out and thousands of helpless people would be killed. Then Cortes promised that if the Aztecs would lay down their arms he would treat them with respect.

But Cuauhtémoc would not listen to proposals for peace. Instead, he ordered stores to be gathered to feed his people during a siege of the capital and sent out a message to all of his subject towns. He wanted them to join him in his battle against the invaders. He promised his allies that if they came with their weapons and fought beside him, he would release them from the heavy burden of paying some of the tribute they had been forced to give since their conquest by the Aztecs.

Seeing that his pleas were ignored, Cortes ordered Sandoval to return to Tlaxcala to bring the fleet to Texcoco. Riding toward Tlaxcala, Sandoval met a long column of eight thousand Tlaxcalan warriors hauling the dismantled sections of the ships, along with new supplies of food, toward Cortes' new base of operations. Martín López had not waited for orders to advance, but he was glad to see Sandoval, knowing that his column would need all possible protection against surprise attacks.

Several days later the column reached Texcoco. From that moment, Cortes and Martín López rushed to reconstruct the small fleet and to build a canal wide enough and deep enough for the ships to be launched in it. The canal, dug with the crude axes and mattocks of the Tlaxcalan laborers, was planned so that it would run straight from the conquistadors' camp to the lake itself. The Aztec war canoes on the lake would thus be prevented from raiding the construction site of the ships, and a degree of secrecy might be preserved. In recent times, traces of this great construction project have been found.

During the months that his Indian allies were working on the fleet, Cortes and his captains set out to subdue those towns bordering the lake that still remained loyal to Cuauhtémoc. The captains moved from town to town.

chalchicueyca

An Indian artist told the story of Cortes' preparations for the 1521 expedition by means of this map. Spanish officers are shown at the bottom of the map dispatching two bearers to Cortes in Tlaxcala and keeping the natives in line at Villa Rica de Vera Cruz. The drowning Indians, left center, may be those caught in the flood at Ixtapalapa.

Sometimes they were accepted with friendly greetings. Sometimes they had to fight their way from house to house. The campaign kept Cortes' men in fighting shape and helped season the new recruits.

While the series of small preparatory campaigns was taking place, a second ship from Spain arrived on the coast. On board was a royal treasurer who had been ordered to keep careful records of the "royal fifth." This was, in effect, acknowledgment from Spain that King Charles was aware of Cortes and knew what was going on in Mexico. While recognition must have been important to Cortes, the large supply of arms and powder that the ship also brought were probably even more welcome. The supplies were quickly transported to Texcoco to be allotted to the troops.

With the ships nearly ready for launching and the long channel that would float them to the lake almost finished, Cortes suddenly found that he was facing a conspiracy against his life. Some of Narváez's men who still remained with Cortes believed that they could now stop dissembling and take action. Secretly, they planned the death of Cortes, Alvarado, Sandoval, and a third captain, Andrés de Tapia.

The plot was a simple one: there was a newly arrived ship at Villa Rica de Vera Cruz to take the conspirators away. All they had to do was kill Cortes and his loyal captains. They planned to do this at dinner, when one of the conspirators would deliver a letter to Cortes. While Cortes was reading the letter he would be stabbed to death. The conspirators were so certain their plan would work that they selected one of their own leaders as the new captain general and passed out other important offices to their friends.

The plot was kept secret for two days after Cortes and his captains returned from campaigning in the countryside. Then one of the soldiers involved in the plot came to Cortes and told him the whole story. Cortes listened and moved quickly. First he briefed his loyal officers, and then he moved to the quarters of the chief conspirator, Antonio de Villafaña. There Cortes and his captains seized several men involved in the plot, and Cortes found a letter on which all of the conspirators had signed their names.

Too many of the names were those of important men whom Cortes still wanted to win over to himself, and so he at once put out the story that Villafaña had swallowed the letter before anyone could read it. The trial that followed was a formality because Villafaña admitted everything. He was summarily hanged from the window of the room where he lived.

When Cortes wrote to King Charles about his preparations for the forthcoming siege, he did not mention this bit of treason or the fact that he had had to hang a man. His own position at court was not yet secure, and he wanted everyone to believe that those with him were loyal.

The spring of 1521 was passing rapidly. More than eight thousand natives from Culhuacan and Texcoco had been employed daily in digging the ship channel. The channel had by this time progressed to the point where it was more than twelve feet deep and just as wide. It had sturdy embankments and was separated from the lake by a small dike. As Cortes wrote the king in Spain: "It was certainly a very great work and worthy of admiration."

On Sunday, April 28, water was let into the channel; the fleet was launched and poled out onto the lake. Then Cortes held a review. He found "eighty-six horsemen, one hundred eighteen crossbowmen and gunners, seven hundred-odd foot soldiers with swords and shields, three heavy iron cannon, fifteen small bronze fieldpieces, and ten-hundred-weight of powder." When the review was over he charged the Spaniards to obey the ordinances that he had set down for the conduct of the war ". . . and to be merry and keep up their courage, for they saw how Our Lord was leading us to victory over our enemies. . . ." He pointed out to them how their forces had grown in the months that

More than ten thousand Indians, led by the Tlaxcala chieftains and the Spaniards under López, hauled the prefabricated ships and other much-needed supplies to Texcoco. In this eighteenth-century print the caravan is shown nearing Lake Texcoco. At far right sawyers make a rudder to be installed at the lake.

had passed. ". . . the principal thing," he said, "was the fact that we were fighting to promote the spread of our faith and to reduce to Your Majesty's service so many rebellious provinces. . . ."

The day after the great review, Cortes sent messages to three allied Indian cities and told their caciques that the fleet had been launched and that he needed their support. He "would wait ten days for them, and they must take no longer." The native allies arrived in time, and Cortes then organized his troops for battle.

I divided them and assigned them to three captains, each of whom with his division was to be stationed in one of three cities around Tenochtitlán. I made Pedro de Alvarado captain of one

TEXT CONTINUED ON PAGE 128

125

In a canal leading to the lake, final assembly of the fleet took place. An illustration from a contemporary history known

as the Durán Atlas shows both Spanish and Tlaxcalan supervisors overseeing construction of several canoelike vessels.

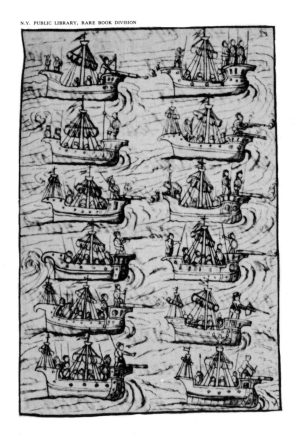

The strangely proportioned map on the opposite page was drawn under the supervision of Cortes and appeared in the Latin edition of his second letter to King Charles. It shows both Mexico City (bottom) and the Gulf of Mexico (at top). Cortes' strategy for taking the Aztecs' capital was a sequence of blockade, siege, and assault: as the first step, his captains were to seize cities like Tacuba (labeled "Atacuba" at the lower right of the map), which guarded the causeways leading into the island capital; later Cortes would sail up with the fleet from Texcoco (off the bottom of the map). Twelve of the fleet's thirteen ships are shown at left in an illustration from the 1585 history called the Florentine Codex. The vessels measured about forty-two feet in length and carried a complement of some twenty-five men.

TEXT CONTINUED FROM PAGE 125

division and assigned him thirty horsemen, eighteen crossbowmen and gunners, and one hundred and fifty foot soldiers, and more than twenty-five thousand warriors of our allies. They were to make their headquarters at Tacuba.

I made Cristóbal de Olid captain of another division . . . the division to make their headquarters in Coyoacán.

Gonzalo de Sandoval was captain of the third division . . . This division was to go to Ixtapalapa and destroy it, then to advance over a causeway, protected by the ships, to join the garrison at Coyoacán.

After I entered the lake with the ships, Sandoval would fix his headquarters where it suited him best.

For the thirteen ships I left three hundred men, almost all of them sailors and well drilled, so that each ship had twenty-five Spaniards, and each of the small vessels had a captain, a pilot, and six crossbowmen and gunners.

On May 10, Alvarado and Olid left Texcoco with their commands. The siege of Tenochtitlán was about to begin. It was to become the longest siege and one of the bloodiest battles in the history of the New World. At its end an entire civilization would be destroyed and the largest city ever found by the conquistadors laid waste.

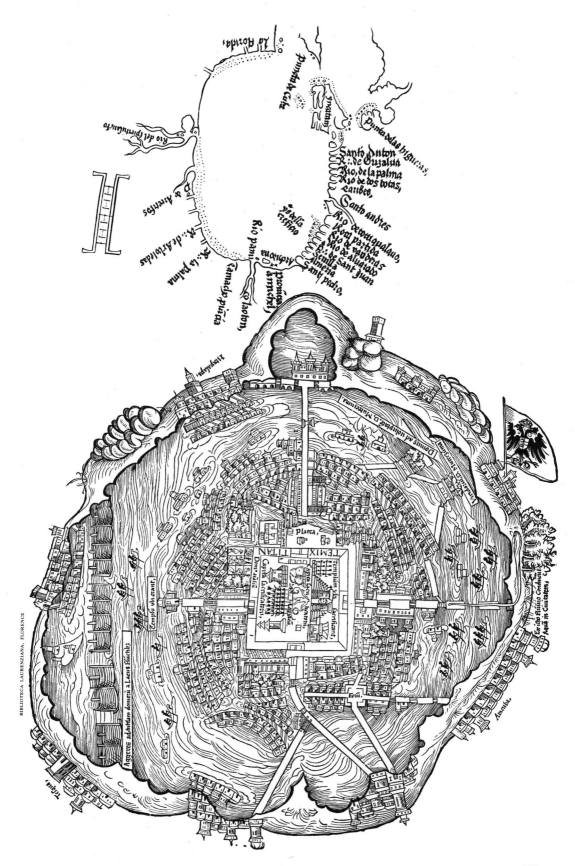

129

VIII   CONQUEST BY WATER

PALACIO DE CORTES, CUERNAVACA

On May 26, the troops under Alvarado and Olid approached the aqueduct that carried water from the springs of Chapultepec to the city. The Aztecs had expected this attack on their water supply and were prepared to meet it. But after a very brief skirmish, they were routed, and the invaders smashed the aqueduct.

The siege had begun. The captains marched to the positions around the capital from which they were to launch their assaults. For the next several days the Aztecs attacked the Spanish emplacements gingerly and probingly—as though feeling out the strength and battle plans of the conquistadors. Later they attacked violently and knowingly, and were repulsed only with great effort.

On May 31 Cortes led his fleet out onto the lake. He had long been convinced that the fleet was the key to victory; now he was out to prove that all of the effort had been worth-while. As the fleet sailed past the small fortress atop the promontory on the southern shore of the lake, a

Commanding his newly built brigantines to sail against the walls of the Aztecs' island capital, Cortes stands with sword upraised in this section of a Diego Rivera mural.

signal was sent out warning the city that the Spanish ships were coming. Furious that his approach had been revealed, Cortes and some companions leaped ashore, scaled the rocky heights, and took the fortress. While he was fighting on the promontory Cortes received word that the Aztec fleet of war canoes had been sighted. Looking down he could see as many as fifteen hundred large canoes advancing toward him on the lake.

Hurrying back to his ship, he waited for the Aztecs to come within the range of his harquebuses and cannon. For a brief moment the Aztec warriors hesitated, unsure of the best way to attack these strange foreign vessels. At the same moment a slow breeze began to blow off the land toward the Spanish fleet. Cortes signaled for his captains to set their sails and prepare for battle while the Indians were still off guard. Under full canvas the small armada headed directly into the mass of Aztec canoes, crushing some, overturning others, and scattering the rest. In a few minutes the waters were churning with swimming or drowning natives trying desperately to climb aboard the few battered canoes that remained afloat or to swim after those racing toward the security of the city.

With the wind in their sails the Spanish ships surged down the lake, creating havoc in all directions with the heavy shot of their cannon and the furious fire of their harquebuses. The few canoes that escaped eventually found safety in the city's network of inlets and small canals where the larger Spanish ships could not pursue them. Cortes was satisfied that he had destroyed the greater part of the Aztec fleet, and he knew that he now held undisputed sway over Mexico's inland sea.

It was almost evening when he began to withdraw his fleet from the fringes of the city. However, his day's work was not yet complete. As he approached the juncture of the great southern causeway, he decided that he must capture the fortress that guarded its landward approaches. Landing with thirty men he made his assault, and though the enemy resisted, he took his objective. Cortes decided that the newly won position was an ideal place for his general headquarters, and he set up camp in the fortress.

Cortes believed the city to be completely surrounded. However, he soon learned that the Tepeyac causeway in the north of the city was still open and that the Aztecs were using it as their main route of supply and escape. The captain general ordered Sandoval to move his troops to Tepeyac to block the causeway. The following day the maneuver was completed, and three hundred thousand warriors were bottled up in Tenochtitlán.

For the first three weeks in June the conquistadors and their Indian allies fought skirmishes on the outskirts of the city. The pattern of attack was similar from day to day. One day the forces of Olid might penetrate farther than those of Pedro de Alvarado, the next day the men under Sandoval might penetrate farther.

The Aztecs fought from behind barricades, from roof tops, and from canoes in the narrow canals that criss-crossed the city. The Spaniards would take a square, then lose it and fall back. Many of the houses on the outskirts of the city were burned, "and not a canoe dared to venture there." Every day the ships captured more canoes and more prisoners. Yet despite the gradual destruction of their forces, the Aztecs showed no signs of surrendering.

Realizing that the enemy was determined to fight to the bitter end, Cortes remarked, ". . . We would recover little if any of the treasure that had been taken from us, and they would force us to destroy them totally. This last caused me the greater sorrow," he said, "because it weighed on my soul."

In preparing for a major assault on the Tenochtitlán, Cortes first ordered his men to burn the residences near the center of the city where they had lived the year before. The attack was swift and successful and took the Aztecs completely by surprise. They had believed that the Spaniards could never penetrate so far into the city.

Two days later, after numerous forays, Cortes entered the city at dawn. He hoped to arrive before the Aztecs had had a chance to repair the canals that the Spaniards had filled with debris the day before. However, the waterways had already been cleared, and passage through the streets was almost impossible. The two forces closed, and the battle was fought hand to hand until the Spaniards had used all their arrows or ammunition and were too exhausted to go on. The only way they could withdraw was to swim across the open gaps where the water flowed through the streets. Slowly, and with heavy losses, the conquistadors found a route and made their way out of the city.

Each day the battle seemed more difficult and victory further away. Each day the invaders had to bridge open streams before they could enter the city. And each night the Indians demolished their work. As Cortes wrote to King Charles in Spain:

Every day the Spaniards gathered new courage and determined

This detail from a large view of the first action on Lake Texcoco shows Cortes' brigantines moving through the grasses offshore to engage a swarm of native canoes.

133

HERNAN CORTES

to cross, for they saw my own resolve and, sink or swim, the thing had to be done. As for placing guards at the bridges by night, we were so weary after fighting all day that it was impossible to do this.

Every effort that Cortes made to break the Aztec hold on the city failed; the Mexicans were determined to remain. Day after day Cortes expected to hear of their surrender, or that the Aztecs had fallen prey to the ambushes he had set for them. But they held firm. Nothing that Cortes could devise seemed to break the Aztecs' spirit.

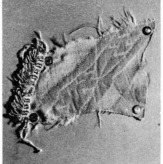

With care he prepared still another assault. This time he planned to bring all of the forces at his command to bear at a single moment. The cities along the lake were ordered to supply what men and canoes they could, the allies were alerted, and all of the Spaniards who could still fight were readied for the assault. Approaching the city from all directions at once, Cortes spread his men over the greater part of it, destroying and burning as he went, completely outmaneuvering the enemy. But as the sun began to set he withdrew his men. He did not yet feel secure enough to camp inside the city, for he knew that the Aztecs would attack all through the night. As his men fell back, Cortes felt that this time nearly three-fourths of the capital was his.

During the continuous forays up and down the causeways, a competitive spirit had developed among Cortes' captains. Each one wanted to penetrate farther into the beleaguered city than his companions. Although Cortes had warned them never to "gain a palm of ground without having the exit and entrance of the horsemen absolutely assured," one day the impetuous Alvarado pressed too far. He allowed his division to enter the city over a partially filled gap in the causeway. When there were only forty or fifty men on the far side of the gap, which was not sufficiently filled to bear the weight of the horses, the Aztec captains ordered their counterattack. Alvarado's men were driven into the water and three or four of them were taken alive for sacrifice. Though this defeat caused Cortes "the greatest sorrow in the world," he was to have still greater cause for sorrow.

On June 13, the anniversary of the *noche triste*, he en-

TEXT CONTINUED ON PAGE 138

Cortes' leadership, and the presence of his standard (a fragment of which is above) in the thick of battle, was the dynamic force that drove the Spaniards forward. The portrait of the captain general is by an unknown artist.

135

This European water color is a copy of a sixteenth-century Aztec picture: in assaulting a cause-

way, Cortes has fallen into the shallow water and is being given a hand by an Indian ally.

TEXT CONTINUED FROM PAGE 135

tered the city once more. Many of his troops had gone before him earlier in the day, and as he rode down a street he saw that his men had crossed over "a ditch in the street that was ten paces broad, with water flowing through it twenty feet deep, and that in passing they had thrown wood and maize and reed grass into it." They had passed a few at a time and with care, and they thought that they had protected their escape route.

Yet no sooner had Cortes reached this "accursed bridge" than he saw his men running in full retreat toward him. He realized immediately that this could mean disaster, and he tried to hold his men back, but the water was already filled with Spaniards and Indians, as though "not one straw had been put into it." The Aztecs in their fury followed the conquistadors into the water, fighting so viciously that Cortes was convinced that he would die at this point.

But the most I and my men could do was lend a hand to some unlucky Spaniards who were drowning. Some came out wounded, and others half drowned and without weapons. I sent them back to the rear. The enemy were so numerous that they soon surrounded me and some ten or fifteen who had remained with me. I was so occupied helping those who were drowning that I had not thought about my own danger until some Indians grabbed me and were on the point of carrying me off.

One Spanish captain and several of his men fought through to help Cortes, and he slowly began to retreat, fighting with his sword and buckler. "At this point a servant rode up on horseback and cleared a little space, but immediately a lance thrown from a low roof struck him in the throat and overthrew him." A second servant succeeded in bringing him a horse, but it was of little use on the muddy causeway. Carefully securing their passage, Cortes and his men withdrew down the causeway under heavy attack by the frantic Aztecs.

When Cortes finally reached safety, he counted his losses. Thirty-five or forty Spaniards and over a thousand allies had been killed. Cortes himself was among the wounded. But the horror of the anniversary of the *noche triste* was not yet over. The Aztecs had captured a number of Spaniards in their battle with Cortes and had taken these prisoners to the far side of the city where Alvarado and his men were camped. Here, the Aztecs raised their prisoners "to the top of some lofty towers, stripped them and opened their breasts, and taking out the hearts, offered them to their idols."

Lienzo de Tlaxcalla, CHAVERO, 1892

teçıquauhtıtlã

Watching from but a short distance away, Alvarado's men recognized their companions. They were stunned and horrified. But the Aztecs, jubilant over their prizes of victory, spent the night in celebration.

In the days that followed, news of the Aztec victory spread through Mexico. Cortes' allies began deserting to their homes. Even those who had stood by him the year before were leaving. Yet despite the loss of many allies, Cortes stood firm. As long as he had enough men to continue the blockade of the city, Cortes knew that time was on his side. The besieged Aztecs would eventually consume everything edible and have to sue for peace. This, at least, was a small comfort to Cortes as he watched the thousands of friendly Indians take the long road back to their towns. Some of them, however, promised to return when he was ready to fight again.

More than fifty-five days had passed since the siege had begun, and still the enemy remained unbeaten. Most of the Spanish ammunition and arrows had been used. Some new supplies were received when a ship put in at Villa Rica de Vera Cruz with the remnants of Ponce de León's expedition that had been routed on the Florida coast.

Two stages of the amphibious assault on Tenochtitlán are noted in this copy of the Tlaxcalan canvas. At top Cortes and Doña Marina arrive by ship at a crucial causeway junction. Below, Doña Marina acts as a shield-bearer while two Spanish soldiers fight their way past a temple where the head of a sacrificial victim is still visible.

The hand-to-hand battles in the streets of Tenochtitlán are recalled in this Rivera mural. Cortes (mounted, lower center) fights alongside an Indian ally. Many Aztec knights wear the skins and headdresses symbolic of their clans. Added to the din of battle is the noise of conch trumpets (upper left).

140

Finally, Cortes and his men had recovered sufficiently to begin attacking once more. This time he was determined that he would never again be trapped as he had been on the causeway. He would leave no roofs for the Aztecs to fight from, no houses for them to hide within, no gaps in the causeways and streets to trap his men. Everything would be razed as the Spaniards moved forward. If need be, the entire city would be leveled, building by building. No stone would remain on another. This was a battle to the end, and Cortes was determined to win it regardless of the cost. Messengers were sent to his allies telling them he was ready to fight again, and many of them rejoined him.

Each day the invaders marched down the causeways, entered the town, and continued their destruction. As the Indian allies tore the buildings apart, Spanish soldiers hid nearby and Spanish horsemen lurked behind the column of soldiers. Invariably the Aztecs took the bait and attacked the invading Indians. Invariably, too, the Spaniards trapped the Aztecs between the hidden soldiers and the cavalry. "With these ambushes," Cortes wrote, "we killed some of them every afternoon."

The Spaniards began to notice signs that the Aztecs were feeling the effects of the siege. At the beginning of the long battle, they had buried their dead with all their accustomed funeral rites. Soon they no longer had time to bury the corpses and merely hid them inside the houses. As the campaign dragged on week after week, they no longer even bothered with their dead. Cut off from the countryside that fed them, the Aztecs were slowly starving. Gnawed roots and the chewed bark of trees were seen in the streets. But still they fought on. The youthful emperor had no intention of surrendering.

Time after time Cortes sent messengers to Cuauhtémoc asking him to abandon the fight, but he always received the same answer, "If there were only one man left, he would die fighting."

The siege went on and on: a clash in one part of the city, a skirmish in another, ambush and retreat; and forever, the death of Spaniards, allies, and Aztecs. Finally, the representatives of the Aztec emperor agreed that Cuauhtémoc would meet with Cortes. The appointed hour came. Cortes was there, but the emperor never appeared— he had apparently realized that the struggle could end in nothing less than his total victory or total defeat. But Cortes took no pride in the slaughter that then ensued; he called the last phase of the siege a "mockery." The Aztecs no longer had the weapons nor the strength to wield them. They were dying of starvation and thirst.

At last Cortes made what he thought was his last assault. The way through the city was open. No one came out to oppose the invaders. And the Indian allies of the Spaniards avenged themselves. "That day they slaughtered and took prisoner more than forty thousand men. The shrieks and the weeping of the women and children was heartbreaking." The Spaniards were too few to control their allies, and they had to countenance sickening cruelty and barbarism.

That night nearly all of the ruined city was in Cortes' hands. The stench of the dead, left lying in the summer heat for days, permeated the island. Men who had fought most of their adult lives were revolted by it and withdrew.

It was already August 12; although there were lulls, the fighting continued, and it appeared that the brutality of constant battle would last through the rest of the summer. On this day Cortes expected to meet with the emperor to receive a petition for surrender; but once more the Aztecs failed to appear as they had promised. The fighting began again and lasted through most of the day. Hoping to avoid another battle, Cortes went to the top of one of the few re-

In the 75-day-long assault on Tenochtitlán in 1520, Cortes' forces literally dismembered the Aztec capital. In the Spanish painting at right, chieftains' heads (indicated by the numbers 41) are displayed from the embattled temple; in the section of the Rivera mural above, a church official supervises the destruction of the great temple and the burning of the Aztec histories.

To insure that no viewer misunderstood this contemporary Aztec painting of the siege of Tenochtitlán, the artist drew a Spaniard (lower left) beneath Cortés' men and an Indian in feathered headdress under Cuauhtémoc's forces.

144

maining buildings and pleaded with the caciques to end the slaughter.

The caciques met together and agreed to parley. For more than five hours the enemies talked. There was so little ground left to the Aztecs that they had to walk on the bodies of their dead. Some of them had withdrawn to the lake where they swam to the far shore or drowned. Cortes noted, "their plight was such it was impossible to conceive how they could endure it."

As the hours passed, Cortes realized that he would have to order a final assault. He fired a shot, the signal to advance, and watched the death agonies of Tenochtitlán.

More than fifty thousand of them perished from salt water they drank, or from starvation and pestilence. . . . As the people of the city came toward us, I ordered Spaniards to be stationed in all the streets to prevent our allies from killing those unhappy people. I also ordered the captains of the allies to restrain their men in every way possible. But our allies were so many we could not prevent a massacre, and that day more than fifteen thousand were killed.

In the late afternoon, the captain of one of the ships stopped an escaping canoe. The men aboard the Spanish craft leveled their guns and prepared to fire when those in the canoe cried out that the emperor was among them.

As soon as Cortes heard that the young Aztec had been taken prisoner, he sent for him. The captain general had his men carpet a terrace with crimson cloth and matting, and he waited for his prisoner to appear. Doña Marina was at his side. As Cuauhtémoc mounted the terrace where Cortes sat, the Spanish leader rose to his feet and stepped forward. For a time both men were silent. Then Cuauhtémoc told Cortes that he had done all that he could to defend himself and his people. Now reduced to his present wretched state, he asked Cortes to deal with him as the conquering Spaniard wished.

Cortes, filled with admiration for the bravery and determination of the young Aztec, told him that he respected valor even in an enemy. He called for Cuauthémoc's wife to join her husband, and in peace at long last, they sat down together.

After seventy-five days, Tenochtitlán had finally been subdued by the persistent Spaniards and abandoned by its people. The war with the Mexicans had come to an end. The Aztec empire had crumbled with the destruction of its great and beautiful city. The breaking of the siege of Tenochtitlán marked the beginning of Spanish rule on the mainland of the New World. Yet the shift from conquerors to colonial administrators did not come easily for most of the officers who had sailed with Cortes. They were not by nature bureaucrats. They had started out as adventurers hoping to find riches and converts for their religion and way of life. But once the adventure was over and the conquest complete, they wanted their share of the spoils of victory.

The Spaniards had fought long and hard; they had almost all been wounded one or more times; they had seen their companions killed on the battlefield or on the altars of the enemy. Now they wanted to be paid, and to the surprise of everyone, including Cortes, there was very little treasure to be found.

No one really knows just what happened to the great treasure amassed before the *noche triste* and abandoned during that fateful night. When Cortes and his men set out to recover it upon their return to the city, only a small part of it could be found. Some of the conquistadors claimed that the Aztecs had taken it out of the city before the siege began. Some claimed that Cortes and his captains actually found it and confiscated it for their own use. Still others believed the story told by some of the Aztec leaders that the treasure had been thrown into the lake to thwart the conquerors. Whatever the answer, only a few golden reminders of the original treasure remained.

The Aztecs nominally continued to rule for a time, with the conquistadors and caciques ruling together under the direction of the Spanish court and the Church. But soon the temptation to use the Indians as slaves became too great to be resisted. Christianity was forgotten as the Indians were herded together, branded, and forced to toil in the gold and silver mines and on the great plantations that were parceled out to the conquerors of New Spain.

While Mexico City was being rebuilt and the country explored and exploited, Cortes waited for word from Spain concerning the legality of his own position. He had notified King Charles of his victory and of the establishment of the new empire, but both Velásquez and the Bishop of Burgos were determined to destroy Cortes.

Finally, the wrangling for power reached such proportions that both the king and the pope entered into the argument. Special committees were established to study the various claims, and the results completely vindicated Cortes. An order went out on October 15, 1522, naming

After the fall of the Aztec capital, the conquistadors rode on to invade other regions of the New World. This detail from a native history shows a Spanish cavalryman on an expedition to Florida.

Cortes governor, captain general, and chief justice of New Spain. At last, after hazarding his life and fortune, he was recognized by his king. With a strong hand, but with love for his adopted land, Cortes ruled until 1534 when Charles made Antonio de Mendoza the viceroy of New Spain, with authority to act with royal power. Cortes retained his titles and rank, but never again was he to wield the power he held at the moment the conquest ended.

He arranged a marriage for Doña Marina to Juan Jaramillo, one of his captains, and then returned for what he thought would be a brief visit to Spain. But when his visit was completed in 1547 and he was on his way to embark for Mexico at the Spanish port of Seville, his great strength began to fail. Within a few days he died—not on a charging horse or in combat on the causeway, but peacefully in bed. His family, knowing that that would have been his wish, moved his body to Mexico.

Today there are no statues of Cortes in the land he conquered; he and his fellow conquistadors have been rejected by more recent generations. But the great civilization that he overcame with steel and courage is remembered everywhere in modern Mexico. Pride in the Aztec past and delight in rediscovery of Aztec culture are strong. The Aztecs who conquered and then were conquered are winning, through history, the final victory.

In 1592, when Theodore de Bry made a map of the New World, New Spain (section above) was a vast area that included the southwestern United States, Mexico, Central America, the West Indies, and great reaches of the Pacific. For all this, Mexico City was the seat of government from 1521 until 1821.

147

PHOTO BY ALICE D. WATSON

For conquering Mexico Cortes was granted a title by King Charles—he became Marquis of Oaxaca Valley. His valley (above) was rich, but it was no substitute for the lost gold.

AMERICAN HERITAGE PUBLISHING CO., INC.

James Parton, *President*

Joseph J. Thorndike, Jr., *Editor in Chief*

Richard M. Ketchum, *Editorial Director, Book Division*

Irwin Glusker, *Art Director*

HORIZON CARAVEL BOOKS

RUSSELL BOURNE, *Editor*

Sean Morrison, *Assistant Editor*

Janet Czarnetzki, *Art Director*

Judith Harkison, *Chief Picture Researcher*

Elaine K. Andrews, *Copy Editor*

Nancy Simon, *Editorial Assistant*

Betsy Sanders, *Editorial Assistant*

Gertrudis Feliu, *Chief, European Bureau*

ACKNOWLEDGMENTS

The Editors are deeply indebted to the staff members of many private and public collections in which paintings, photographs, and articles of special importance to this book were found. Foremost among these collections are the Museo Nacional de Antropologia and the Museo Nacional de Historia in Mexico City; the Biblioteca Nacional and Museo Naval in Madrid; and the New York Public Library, American History and Rare Book divisions. In addition, the Editors wish to thank the following individuals and organizations for their assistance and for making available material in their collections:

Dr. A. Arriaga, Director, Museo Nacional de Historia, Mexico, D.F.

Mr. Calatayud, Superintendent, Chapultepec Castle, Mexico, D.F.

Dr. Cortina Goribar, Instituto Nacional de Antropologia e Historia, Mexico, D.F.

Mrs. Icaza de Xirau, Director, City of Mexico Art Gallery

Mr. Lino Picaseño, Curator, San Carlos Art Library, Mexico, D.F.

Don José López de Toro, Curator, Don Ramón Paz of the Manuscript Section, and the Fine Arts Section, Biblioteca Nacional, Madrid

Admiral Julio Guillén, Curator, and Lieut. Commander Roberto Barreiro-Meiro, Museo Naval, Madrid

Barbara J. Price, Adelphi University

Frederick J. Dockstader, Director, Museum of the American Indian

Special research and photography: Mexico—Joseph Hefter, Fernando Lipkau; Spain—Jane Horton de Cabanyes; Italy—Maria Todorow

148

FURTHER REFERENCE

Readers interested in further examining artifacts of the conquistadors and of Spain's early colonial period will find collections of varying kinds in the following museums: American Museum of Natural History, New York City; Arizona State Museum, University of Arizona, Tucson; Chicago Natural History Museum; Museum of New Mexico, Santa Fe; Peabody Museum of Archaeology and Ethnology, Harvard University; University Museum, University of Pennsylvania; Middle American Research Institute, Tulane University; and Robert H. Lowie Museum of Anthropology, University of California, Berkeley.

For those who wish to read further on Cortes, the Aztecs, and the conquest of Mexico, the following books are recommended:

Blacker, Irwin R. and Rosen, Harry M. *The Golden Conquistadors*. The Bobbs-Merrill Co., 1960.

Coe, Michael D. *Mexico*. Frederick A. Praeger, 1962.

Cortes, Hernando. *Five Letters of Cortes to the Emperor*. W. W. Norton Co., 1962.

Covarrubias, Miguel. *Indian Art of Mexico and Central America*. Alfred A. Knopf, 1957.

Díaz del Castillo, Bernal. *The Discovery and Conquest of Mexico*. Translated by A. P. Maudslay. Grove Press, 1956.

Gardiner, C. Harvey. *Naval Power in the Conquest of Mexico*. University of Texas Press, 1956.

Gillmor, Frances. *Flute of the Smoking Mirror*. The University of New Mexico Press, 1949.

Gómara, Francisco López de. *Cortes*. Translated by Lesley Byrd Simpson. University of California Press, 1964.

Haring, C. H. *The Spanish Empire in America*. Harcourt, Brace & World, 1963.

Kubler, George. *The Art and Architecture of Ancient America*. Penguin Books, 1962.

Parkes, Henry Bamford. *A History of Mexico*. Houghton Mifflin Co., 1960.

Peterson, Frederick A. *Ancient Mexico*. G. P. Putnam's Sons, 1959.

Prescott, William H. *History of the Conquest of Mexico and the Conquest of Peru*. The Modern Library, n.d.

Robertson, Donald. *Pre-Columbian Architecture*. George Braziller, Inc., 1963.

Sedgwick, Henry Dwight. *Cortes the Conquerer*. The Bobbs-Merrill Co., 1926.

Soustelle, Jacques. *The Daily Life of the Aztecs*. The Macmillan Co., 1962.

Thompson, J. Eric. *The Rise and Fall of the Maya Civilization*. University of Oklahoma Press, 1954.

Vaillant, George C. *The Aztecs of Mexico*. Penguin Books, 1960.

Von Hagen, Victor Wolfgang. *The Ancient Sun Kingdoms of the Americas*. The World Publishing Co., 1961.

Wolf, Eric. *Sons of the Shaking Earth*. University of Chicago Press, 1962.

INDEX

Bold face indicates pages on which maps or illustrations appear.
Pronunciation of Indian words is given in parentheses.